# Walt Disney

*A Captivating Guide to the Life of an American Entrepreneur and Pioneer of Animated Cartoon Films*

© **Copyright 2020**

This document is geared towards providing exact and reliable information in regard to the topic and issue covered. The publication is sold with the idea that the publisher is not required to render accounting, officially permitted, or otherwise, qualified services. If advice is necessary, legal or professional, a practiced individual in the profession should be ordered.

- From a Declaration of Principles which was accepted and approved equally by a Committee of the American Bar Association and a Committee of Publishers and Associations.

In no way is it legal to reproduce, duplicate, or transmit any part of this document in either electronic means or in printed format. Recording of this publication is strictly prohibited and any storage of this document is not allowed unless with written permission from the publisher. All rights reserved.

The information provided herein is stated to be truthful and consistent, in that any liability, in terms of inattention or otherwise, by any usage or abuse of any policies, processes, or directions contained within is the solitary and utter responsibility of the recipient reader. Under no circumstances will any legal responsibility or blame be held against the publisher for any reparation, damages, or monetary loss due to the information herein, either directly or indirectly.

Respective authors own all copyrights not held by the publisher.

The information herein is offered for informational purposes solely, and is universal as so. The presentation of the information is without contract or any type of guarantee assurance.

The trademarks that are used are without any consent, and the publication of the trademark is without permission or backing by the trademark owner. All trademarks and brands within this book are for clarifying purposes only and are the owned by the owners themselves, not affiliated with this document.

# Free Bonus from Captivating History (Available for a Limited time)

Hi History Lovers!

Now you have a chance to join our exclusive history list so you can get your first history ebook for free as well as discounts and a potential to get more history books for free! Simply visit the link below to join.

Captivatinghistory.com/ebook

Also, make sure to follow us on Facebook, Twitter and Youtube by searching for Captivating History.

# Contents

INTRODUCTION .................................................................................... 1
CHAPTER 1: HUMBLE BEGINNINGS ................................................ 4
CHAPTER 2: THE FIRST STEP ............................................................ 13
CHAPTER 3: THE INDEPENDENT MOVE ........................................ 20
CHAPTER 4: NEW LEAF ..................................................................... 28
CHAPTER 5: BRUSH WITH BANKRUPTCY .................................... 35
CHAPTER 6: HELLO TO HOLLYWOOD .......................................... 44
CHAPTER 7: FAMOUS IN LA ............................................................. 54
CHAPTER 8: FORAY INTO THE BIG LEAGUES ............................. 60
CHAPTER 9: THE BIRTH OF MICKEY MOUSE .............................. 68
CHAPTER 10: DISNEY MOVIE MAGIC ............................................ 77
CHAPTER 11: DISNEY, THE MEGABRAND .................................... 85
CONCLUSION ...................................................................................... 89
FOR FUTURE READING .................................................................... 92

# Introduction

A man truly lives on even after his death if he leaves a legacy that survives him for years to come. Albert Einstein, Harriet Tubman, Karl Marx, Mozart, Marie Curie, Van Gogh, Marsha Johnson—there are so many examples of men and women whose deeds revolutionized history and paved the way for future generations to thrive. One name that stands out in this regard in the world of entertainment is that of Walt Disney. He may not have been a pioneer per se of animation or films, but he was more like the Shakespeare of his genre—he took inspiration from here, there, and everywhere, and he punched it together to create something that is relevant even today.

But do not be mistaken. His contributions are not restricted to the world of films. You will be surprised to learn that he was involved in American history more intimately than any other man working in showbiz. He had been involved in war and peace, politics, and the Olympics, and of course, who hasn't heard of Disney World? He was a man who did not have the word "limit" in his dictionary. He dreamed big dreams and didn't rest until he achieved them. He spread his influence far and wide, and there was not a single discipline he did not dabble in. You name it, and he was there at some point or another. The best thing about this man was that he might have been a shy and reserved person in his personal life, but he never shied away from any opportunity that presented itself to him. He knew what the great American Dream was about, and he lived it like a true American.

Walt Disney did not know how to back down. There was a point in his life when everybody was leaving his side. Any person he tried to lean on promptly abandoned him for greener pastures. He was being strong-armed, blackmailed, and manipulated into living life on others' terms, but every time someone punched him down, he would rise back up and create something bigger and better from what he had. Such resilience is only seen in the best of the best.

Disney was also all for the future. He was a proponent of new technologies, newer methods, and the newest inventions. He tried and tested everything before choosing the diamond from the coal. Disney was nothing if not thorough; he is even known to have sent his staff to institutions to learn the latest developments in the fields they worked in. One story goes that he made his men tour the whole country to assess the pros and cons of every amusement park in the country before he built his own. You have to give it to the man for his perfectionism and eye for excellence in everything he did.

Although Walt Disney created the entertainment empire we know today, he had quite a tragic end to his life. While he had started smoking as a young man, he became a chain smoker around the time of World War I. It had been stressful times, and smoking was probably the only coping mechanism he knew. But while it gave temporary solace to Walt's mind, it totally devastated his body. He was diagnosed with lung cancer in late November of 1966, and although he attempted to treat it with the latest treatments, he died not even a month after. Perhaps he did not have many regrets, as he had done much and accomplished so many of his dreams. But it is not hard to realize that he did regret the fact that he did not live to see his biggest dream come true. His plans to set up a futuristic town never materialized in his lifetime, but Walt Disney World did come to life a few years after his death.

Disney's life was not devoid of controversy, though. At various times in his life and after his death, he had been accused of racism and anti-Semitism. He has also been criticized for propagating ethnocentric notions and being a hooded supporter of America's attempts at enforcing cultural imperialism around the world, especially in Europe. He had a bad reputation for being a tough, ruthless, obsessive boss that made his employees work relentlessly to realize his vision. But these complaints are highly debatable since, while some have made these claims, others had, simultaneously, refuted them in a vocal manner and ardently supported Disney. While there is no open evidence to back up these claims, Disney's works do undoubtedly have an undercurrent of occidental superiority and insensitivity toward other races and cultures running through them. Whether the individual is to be blamed here or the normativity attached to such callousness in those times is for the reader to decide. But it can, under no circumstance, be denied that Walt Disney was truly a cultural icon, whose revolutionary ideas and vision were exemplary and far too advanced for the times.

# Chapter 1: Humble Beginnings

On December 5th, 1901, the fourth of five children of Elias and Flora Disney was born in their 1249 Tripp Avenue home in the Hermosa neighborhood of Chicago, Illinois. This boy was named Walter Elias Disney. Walt's father, Elias, was the eldest among eleven children of Irish Protestants Kepple and Mary Disney, who had migrated from Ireland to Canada in their childhood. Flora, on the other hand, was of German and English descent through her mother Henrietta and father Charles Call, respectively. She was the sixth among eight daughters of her parents, who also had two sons. The families of Elias and Flora had been neighbors while living in Florida, and the two got married on January 1st, 1888, in Kismet, Florida, which was not far from the plot where Disney World would eventually be built.

Elias had always been a strict, religious man, the kind that would probably be called fanatical nowadays. During Elias' stint as a building contractor in Hermosa, he built the St. Paul Congregational Church. In fact, he had been a trustee in the church while his wife had been the treasurer there. One of the preachers at this church was Walter Parr, an Englishman who was a minister there from 1900 to 1905, and with whom Elias had a cordial relationship. It was after Parr that Elias had named his fourth son Walter. Walter had been the second Disney child to be born at their Tripp Avenue address—Elias and Flora's eldest son, Herbert, had been born at their past address of Acron, Florida, which no longer exists and is a ghost town now, while their second son, Raymond, had been born at their previous home in the Fourth Ward, which is also in Chicago, about two miles west of Lake Michigan. Walt's elder brother and later partner in his enterprise, who was the third child of the brood, Roy Oliver Disney, as well as the youngest child and their only sister, Ruth, was born at Hermosa like Walt himself.

In April 1906, when Walt was four years old and almost two and a half years after Ruth was born, the family moved to Marceline, Missouri, because Elias was apprehensive about the growth of the crime rate in the neighborhood and wanted his kids to grow up free from such influences. In fact, the involvement of two their neighbor's boys, who were in their mid-teens, about the same age as Walt's two eldest brothers, in a car robbery and the subsequent shooting and killing of a cop, which landed one of them with life imprisonment and the other with twenty years of time, was what triggered Elias to make such a decision.

Marceline is about six hours from Chicago, and it was also home to the farm of Elias' younger brother Robert, who helped Elias out with his finances for a long part of his youth. Elias bought a forty-acre farm that had belonged to American Civil War veteran William E. Crane for $3,000 on March 5th, and on April 3rd, he added the five-acre plot that had belonged to the widowed Mrs. Crane for another $450. Living in Marceline was a huge influence on Walt's life because it was here that his artistic flair started to express itself. It started when the boy was asked by a retired doctor in the neighborhood he called Doc Sherwood to draw a picture of his horse Rupert. Sherwood was a part of the group of seniors that Walt loved to hang out with.

Walt began honing his skills by reproducing the cartoons of Ryan Walker, an American activist and cartoonist, from the front page of the *Appeal to Reason* newspaper that his father subscribed to. Walt also taught himself to draw and paint with watercolors and crayons. Soon, he was painting pictures and selling them to other neighbors and family friends. This was Walt's first taste of business. In a way, Walt held the paintbrush before he held a pen because it was only in 1909 that he was first admitted to a school, alongside his sister Ruth. They attended Park School, located in Marceline itself, which had been newly opened in 1908.

Marceline was a town that had cropped up around the Atchison, Topeka, and Santa Fe Railway, which ran through it. Trains had always been a dominating presence in the life of Walt's father, Elias, and it equally influenced Walt. After all, at that time, the market for automobiles was still in its infancy. Marceline itself only had two of them. Walt was obsessed with trains in his childhood, a passion that continued well into adulthood. He would often put his ears on the rail track to listen to the sound of the approaching train. His other uncle, Michael Martin, who was related to the family through his marriage with Walt's mother's elder sister, was a Santa Fe railway engineer who worked on the train route between Fort Madison, Iowa, and Marceline. Walt would look out for him on the trains that arrived.

In 1908, Walt's elder brothers, Herbert and Raymond, ran away from home and moved back to Chicago. This was primarily due to two reasons. Firstly, country life did not agree with them, and secondly, they did not like their father's ways of running the house, as he would make the boys work for him in a fashion that often left them unable to pursue their own interests. So, one night, in the fall of 1908, they escaped through the window of their shared first-floor bedroom. They fled to freedom and later took day jobs as clerks in Kansas City, where they finally ended up.

Soon, however, the rest of the family had to leave, too. Walt's father fell seriously ill when he came down with typhoid fever and then pneumonia. He could no longer maintain the expansive 45-acre farm and had to sell it on November 28$^{th}$, 1910. They first set up in a rented home in Marceline until they could find a better option elsewhere. This came in 1911, when, on May 17th, they found another rented house in Kansas City, Missouri. Coincidentally, or not, Robert Disney was also living in Kansas City at that time. The Disney family stayed there for three years until things looked up again, and they once more got their own house, albeit a modest one, which was also in Kansas City, sometime in September 1914.

Moving to Kansas City started a new phase in the life of Walt, and along with him, Roy. Elias' business itch struck again, and he bought a newspaper delivery route in the city on July 1st, 1911. The paper route had been bought in Roy's name for $2,100. It consisted of two papers, the *Kansas City Star* and the *Kansas City Times*. The *Kansas City Star* was a Sunday and evening newspaper, while the *Kansas City Times* was a morning one. Elias assigned Walt and Roy to be his newspaper delivery boys, and the brothers had to get up as early as 4:30 a.m. every day to deliver the morning paper. They then went to school and would again set off in the evening at 4 p.m. to deliver the evening paper. It was an extremely strenuous job since the *Kansas City Times* had around 700 subscribers, while the *Kansas City Star* had over 600. This number only increased over time. Elias also got dairy and eggs brought in directly from Marceline to be sold to his customers along the route as well. But the two boys never got to keep any of the money. Their father was of the opinion that they were too young to know how to keep or spend money correctly.

Elias had always had an entrepreneurial bent of mind, something that he passed on to Walt. The difference between them, however, laid in the fact that Elias was severely socialist, literally to a fault, while Walt was unabashedly capitalist. So, while Elias' beliefs directly clashed with his attempts at establishing his own business and caused his own failure each time he started out on a venture, Walt's open mind and opportunistic eye caused him to succeed and establish himself. The only quality of his father's that passed onto him and that actually did him any good was Elias' persistence and dogged determination in achieving a goal. Walt had also learned never to be satisfied with what he had and to look for greener pastures from his father.

However, in no way was Elias an ideal parent to his sons. In fact, from the testimonies of his own sons, Elias could easily be classified as an abusive parent, a combined result of the usual parent-child dynamics prevalent at that time and his own authoritarian control. He would often flog and beat up his sons, was infamous for his short temper and flying rages, and expected them to obey him blindly; any disobedience was tagged as a travesty of the child's duties, something that deserved severe punishment. More often than not, Walt, who was a rebellious kid, would lash out at his father from his own impatience with his father's tunnel vision that he inconsiderately tried to burden his sons with. This often caused the atmosphere to get explosive at home and could only be defused by Flora, something that made Walt way closer to his mother than his father.

Elias was also a very stringent Christian. His unwaveringly conservative theism was evident from the rigidly orthodox sermons that he often delivered at church on Sundays. Many believed his religious beliefs were at stark odds with his socio-economic ones. But, as stated earlier, Elias was a bit too socialist for his own good. He used socialism as a safety net to justify his failures, blaming the corrupt machine of the economy rather than his own shortcomings. Elias had, at different times, held an eclectic variety of jobs and often tried his hand at self-employment. He had worked on his father's farm, in a railroad machine shop, with the crew constructing the Union Pacific Railroad in Colorado, a fiddle player, a mailman, an orange grower, a construction worker, a carpenter, a building constructor, and had owned newspaper routes and owned stocks in a jelly canning factory.

He had involved his sons Roy and Walt in his newspaper distribution business, making them work around school. While this often hampered their studies, it is from this that both of them learned to have strong work ethics and the importance of never trying to stop growing and getting better. But simultaneously, Walt's personality differed widely from his father's. While his father was quick to abandon any project, blaming the system for his downfalls, Walt would fight tooth and nail for his creations. Even when they were taken from him, he would reinvent them and make them more successful than his competitors could, a quality that ultimately gave birth to the ubiquitously popular character Mickey Mouse.

But it would be wrong to say that Elias' sons, especially Walter and Roy, whose testimonies are more documented due to their time in the spotlight, hated their father, who they believed was a fiercely protective family man underneath his tough disciplinarian exterior. Having worked in close conjunction with him, Walt believed that, his harsh views and unyielding manner aside, whatever Elias did was to ensure that the family survived. While working on the newspaper route might have hampered Walt's studies to an extent, he kept working not just because telling his father off might have had dire consequences. Walt firmly thought his father only wanted the family to stay afloat since they had been through some trying times financially, and it would be a shame to give up a chance at a comfortable life when they had the opportunity for one. And if he could, Walt would help out.

Walt believed that in spite of being unrelenting in his views and decisions, Elias was essentially a good, moral, and affectionate man, who was only doing what was best for his brood. In contrast, Flora was a comforting presence in Walt's life. She was the indulging parent, who would protect her children from their father's temper and frugality. Walt and Roy went on to recount how their father hated if they took from the dairy or poultry products he had brought in to sell. But their mother always found ways to pamper the children behind her husband's back. In one instance, when conditions used to be tight, their mother would cover slices of bread with butter for the kids, even though Elias had forbidden it, considering it to be a loss for the business. So, to keep it from him, she would coat only one side and then turn it over, effectively hiding the buttered side from him. All the brothers also agreed that Walt was still allowed the greatest amount of slack by their father, as he could at least talk back without receiving the stick. In fact, Walt, being the youngest son, was the darling of the household. Roy, too, was extremely caring toward both his younger siblings. He always indulged them and bought them things, even though he himself was a young boy who hardly had any money.

When the family first moved to Kansas City, both Walt and Ruth were admitted into the Benton Grammar School in 1911, which was near their home. He had to retake the second grade here, in spite of having completed it at his Marceline school. At Benton, he met Walter Pfeiffer. The Pfeiffer family were aficionados of theater, vaudeville, and motion films, and this sparked an interest in Walt for the moving and performing arts, so much so that he often ended up spending more time in the Pfeiffer household than his own. They often took both the kids to theaters to perform skits they wrote, acting in them themselves on amateur nights. Things turned pretty hectic during this time, as their father was making them work for his newspaper now, and Walt often ended up falling asleep at school. As a consequence, this was affecting his grades. He was only nine when he started school here while Roy was eighteen.

This meant that Roy graduated the next year, i.e., in 1912, from the Manual Training High School, and he stopped working for his father. He worked a summer job on his uncle's farm until he got a real job as a clerk with the First National Bank of Kansas City. Elias got other boys to work for him, and he paid them three or four dollars every week. But Walt was denied this because, apparently, he was too young to handle money, and it was part of his responsibility to his family anyway. Elias argued that since he was already taking care of all of the needs a boy like Walt could have, he did not need the extra money. So, as it happens with any kid with irrationally controlling parents, Walt began to go behind his father's back.

While he was delivering the papers, Walt began delivering medicines to the customers of a drugstore. He even went so far as to order more newspapers, over and above what his father did, and selling them to people without his father's knowledge. Not only that, before Roy left, they had also opened a pop stand. This went on for three weeks, and the profits had soon been spent by them. Then Walt started drawing caricature cartoons in the Benton Barber Shop for its owner, Bert Hudson. He was, alongside school and jobs, pursuing his passion for the arts, taking Saturday courses with the Kansas City Art Institute, as well as taking a correspondence course on cartooning.

On March 17th, 1917, Elias sold the paper route because he had better plans in the city of Chicago. Elias had been investing in the stocks of a jelly company in the city, called O-Zell Company, since 1912, and he wanted to get closer to the business so he could have a bigger hand in its management. He was simply waiting for his two youngest children to graduate from the seventh grade in Benton, which they did on June 8th, 1917. But, even though Elias, Flora, and Ruth moved to Chicago, Walt did not. Instead, he continued working for the new owners of the paper route. He stayed in the family home with Roy and the family of his eldest brother Herbert, which included his wife and their infant daughter, Dorothy. It is not hard to speculate that this move on the part of Walt was to get free from the strings of Elias and enjoy a life of greater freedom. Walt took the job of a news butcher, someone who sold items on trains, with the Van Noy Interstate Company, which was based in Kansas and operated on most of the railroads in the country.

This job entailed the vending of various food items, like fruits, snacks, candies, and soft drinks on trains. The job required one to be at least sixteen, but since Walt would not be so until December of that year, he lied about his age and took it anyway. However, Walt was horrible at his new job, which he admitted himself. His introvert nature caused people to steal his empty soda bottles, colleagues to put their own rotten fruits with his stock, and his own gluttony made him eat the candies and snacks he was supposed to sell. This caused his books to not match at the end of the day when he was called for accounting, and every time, Roy paid for the losses Walt thus incurred. The job obviously did not agree with Walt, so he left it as the summer ended and moved in with his parents in Chicago.

The apartment the Disney family had taken in Chicago was in a two-story apartment building on the Near West Side. Here, he became a worker in the jelly factory that Elias had invested in. His work was miscellaneous, as he did daily monotonous jobs, like washing bottles and crushing apples; as well as more daring ones, like being on night watch duty. He also joined the eighth grade at McKinley High School. He took photography and art classes here and soon became the cartoonist of the school newspaper. "The Voice" was one such cartoon that he would publish in the monthly school newspaper. There was an undercurrent of patriotism in his creations, finding inspiration from the subject of the First World War that was going on at that time. He was also taking night classes thrice a week at the Chicago Academy of Fine Arts. In 1918, he was hired at the Chicago Post Office as a mail sorter and substitute mail carrier. Here, too, the trick had been to wear clothes that belonged to his father and lie about his age. He worked here in the daytime from July to September while simultaneously doing the odd job of loading trains at rush hours in the afternoon as a gateman.

# Chapter 2: The First Step

Roy had enlisted in the United States Navy on June 22$^{nd}$, 1917, after the United States joined the ongoing war. Walt loved how his brother looked in the uniform when he would come to visit and made up his mind to enlist as well. In 1918, during the summer, Walt decided to quit school and tried joining the United States Army but was rejected right away as he was underage. Finally, he got a hold of a subscription form for the Red Cross and signed up to be an ambulance driver for the American Ambulance Corps. However, once again, he turned out to be underage for the post. Since the form required the signatures of both his parents, and since his father, due to his Christian values, would not lie in speech or on paper, his mother signed for both of them.

Walt then forged his birth year on the affidavit, changing it from 1901 to 1900, so that he would appear to be of age when obtaining his passport. He had signed up in September, but after coming come down with severe flu in the great 1918 epidemic, his departure was pushed back to November. By the time he reached France on December 4$^{th}$, the armistice had already been signed, and the war was over. But Walt still stayed on for almost a year with the military motor pool, driving the ambulance in France and Germany whenever he was called for. Here, too, his experience with his colleagues was not what he would prefer to call pleasant, but he got by. Perhaps what got him through was the fact that instead of having a camouflage skin for his ambulance, he drew imaginary cartoon characters over any white space he could find on the body of the car. Some of these cartoons were published in the army newspaper called *Stars and Stripes*. He also submitted many of his cartoons to more light-hearted magazines, like *Judge* and *Life*, for publishing. More often than not, he got rejected, but he did make some money out of decorations and caricatures he did for the men in his unit.

In the fall of 1919, Walt finally returned home to Chicago. Roy had also been discharged from service and was now working as a bank teller in Kansas City. Walt rejected the job that had been offered to him by the jelly factory, which paid $25 a week. He no longer wanted to be a menial laborer under his father, doing back-breaking work. Instead, he moved back to Kansas City and lived in the Kansas City family home with Roy and Herbert's family.

Walt tried getting a job with the *Kansas City Star*, which he remembered used to have cartoonists that he often hung out with when he used to be their delivery boy. But there were no openings in the art department, and ironically, he also couldn't get the job of an office boy because the hirers thought he looked a bit too rugged and old for the job. Walt did not have to sit at home for too long, though. Soon, in October of 1919, a colleague at Roy's bank informed him about an apprenticeship post for an advertising cartoonist at the Pesmen-Rubin Commercial Art Studio. The job entailed doing commercial illustrations for clients, like catalogs, advertisements, and banners. Walt showed the owners of the studio, Louis A. Pesmen and Bill Rubin, some of his earlier work, which had been done in France, as samples, and he got the job.

The pay was not decided right away, but a week later, Bill came to Walt and, somewhat indecisively, offered to pay him $50 per month for his work. Walt was elated, especially since he was almost sure that he was about to be sacked. However, this job lasted only for around six weeks. The studio no longer had any work befitting the post, and so, they gave Walt his pink slip. But this job did Walt some good. It launched him in the world of commercial art and illustration. Up until then, he had only drawn for his own pleasure. But doing it commercially not only taught him to manage time better but also taught him the ropes of a job that had a large number of tips and tricks up its sleeve that were necessary for success.

Walt met and befriended Ubbe Iwwerks, known better as Ub Iwerks, at Pesmen-Rubin. It was an association that would prove extremely valuable to Disney in the initial part of his career. Ub worked as a letterer for the company, and he, too, had been dismissed when the company ran out of work. Now, while Walt had a family to support him and had also found work at the post office again, due to the Christmas season, Ub was not so lucky. He had his mother to support, as his father had left her, and he was still jobless. It was in that state that Ub came to visit his friend one day, complaining about his condition. Walt had already been planning to set up his own art business, experimenting with samples to start with, and decided to include Ub in his venture.

So, he suggested that they start a business together. Ub was hesitant at first because he had no money to invest, but Disney had money from his savings that he kept with his parents, who still lived in Chicago, which he intended to use to get them off the ground. So, Iwerks came on board. Walt had his parents send over half of the $500 he had left with them. Even though his father had an entrepreneurial spirit and his mother had always supported him, they were reluctant about Walt using up his savings for his venture, perhaps because he did not have a backup plan and was essentially using up his only capital for an enterprise in a still highly volatile market. But they respected his son's wishes. Walt used the money to buy basic supplies like furniture, airbrushing equipment, drawing supplies, and drawing boards. They named their company Iwerks-Disney Commercial Artists instead of Disney-Iwerks, as Iwerks was pronounced very similar to "eye works," which made it sound like it had something to do with optics.

They first set up the studio in an unused bathroom in the headquarters building of the Restaurant Association, which had been given to them when Walt had gone looking for a business with Alvin Buell Carder, who was, at the time, the secretary of the association. Alvin gave them office space in the bathroom in exchange for artwork for ten dollars a week. Coincidentally, Alvin's parents had been neighbors of the Disneys at their Kansas City home since 1914. The business was modest, and the next assignment came from another of the Disneys' neighbors, the Pfeiffers. The patriarch of the family, John, was the general secretary and treasurer of the leather workers' union United Brotherhood of Leather Workers, and he got the duo to work for them. As a result, the two earned a revenue of $135 in the first month, which was much higher than that at Pesmen-Rubin, allowing them to move to a more dignified location at the Railway Exchange Building. But they still didn't earn enough to make it a profitable business.

So, when Walt came across an advertisement toward the end of June in the *Kansas City Times* and the *Kansas City Star*, which had been put up by the Kansas City Slide Company, for a cartoonist to create slides for them, Disney decided to try and sell them the services of his company and take them on as his customer. However, the Slide Company made him a counter-offer. The owner of the company, Arthur "Vern" Cauger, had and would employ many of the future cartoon industry veterans, the most notable being Joseph Benson Hardaway, also known as Buggsy Hardaway, the creator of Bugs Bunny. Others were Red Lyon, Fred and Hugh Harman, Max Maxwell, Friz Freleng, and George "Jimmy" Lowerre, who would go on to teach Walt stop-motion animation in spite of being cold to him at first. Cauger asked Walt to join his company for forty dollars a week to make slides for local businesses, which was a form of movie theater advertisements quite prevalent in the Midwestern states in those days. Since Disney and Iwerks were not making as much as they had hoped for with their own company, it was decided by both that Disney would work for this company to help bring in some extra money that they could use for their own, while Iwerks would stay back to keep Iwerks-Disney Commercial Artists running.

About the time Walt joined the Kansas City Slide Company, there was a change in it. Wanting to stay on par with the times, the Kansas City Slide Company was renamed as the Kansas City Film Ad Company, as it transitioned from making slides as its main product to making filmed advertisements of short duration. Their office was also shifted from its original location when Disney had joined to a larger premises around February of 1920. However, Ub did not have the business prowess, gift of gab, or entrepreneurial instinct of Walt. As a result, he failed to keep their business afloat by himself, and the very next month, he also joined the Kansas City Film Ad Company.

When Walt had joined the ad company, it was using a form of animation called cut-out animation, which can be considered the early, two-dimensional form of the stop-motion animation technique. In this method, characters, backgrounds, and props are made of cut-outs of some stiff material, with moving parts held by rivets and moved frame by frame. However, being an inquisitive man, Disney was not satisfied with this method, which was the earliest type used in animated films. He started reading books from the local Kansas City Public Library. The most notable ones were *Animated Cartoons: How They Are Made, Their Origin and Development*, written by Edward Lutz and published in February 1920, as well as a book brought to him by Iwerks from the library, *Animals in Locomotion*, a compilation of the photographs of Eadweard Muybridge, a photographer best known for pioneering the idea of stop-motion animation via timed photography and a projector-like contraption called the zoopraxiscope, which he had built. Lutz's book was a very basic one, but it gave Disney the idea of animation using drawings, which was a well-known method and had been prevalent in theater programs since around the year 1915. This method was known as cel animation. In this, every frame was divided into several layers of background, foreground, the characters, and any other moving part of the scene. These layers were hand-drawn on individual transparent celluloid plates, hence why it is called "cel" animation. The layers with unmoving parts were drawn on single plates, while the moving parts were drawn frame by frame and photographed.

The fact that Lutz had proposed that instead of just the background, the parts of a character that were not going to move for a set of scenes should also get a single celluloid plate inspired Disney, who was always on the lookout for cost-effective and effort-saving methods to get work done. He also made Photostat copies of Muybridge's photographs on very thin films to try out the cel process himself. Adding a few tricks and modifications of his own, Walt presented his ideas to Cauger, who gave a positive response. But for all the improvements Walt had envisioned for the company, he did not find any actual takers. People in every stratum of the company, including the manager of the art department, the copywriters, the low-tier supervisors, as well as the cameramen, reacted defensively to Disney's attempts to introduce these changes, which ranged from wariness to outright resistance. Even Cauger, whose reaction had been somewhat favorable, was still reluctant to actually apply the cel method in his company. This frustrated Walt, who decided to try things out by himself. So, in early 1921, he convinced Cauger to let him borrow an old, unused camera of the Kansas City Film Ad Company that was just lying there. Walt planned to use it to experiment and tinker with techniques at the garage of his family home. Cauger was not very eager to let one of his employees, and quite a prized one at that, try to innovate on his own, as he feared Walt might defect, but he allowed it anyway.

Now, there had been changes in the Disney household that allowed Walt to make such a decision. When the O-Zell Company, where Elias had bought stakes, went bankrupt, Elias lost all of his money and was once again a failed man. So, he returned to the Kansas City house around mid-1920 and became a carpenter again, albeit a retired one. Their house did not have a garage to start with; in fact, they did not even have a car. But Elias built one after he returned, as he wanted to earn money by renting it out to other automobile owners. However, Walt came around and set up his workspace in the garage. Walt never paid rent for taking up the garage, even though he had promised five dollars a month. He set up there with the camera and other instruments from the Film Ad Company, with some help from Roy. Walt used to return late from work and would stay up late into the night, working with various animation methods and styles and putting his own twists on them. It was at this makeshift studio that he created the early sample works that he was to take with him when he moved to Hollywood. Basically, Walt Disney was a self-taught animator, and his ability to see the future took him much further than his meager skill and talent could have alone.

# Chapter 3: The Independent Move

Not everything that came out of this makeshift studio was rudimentary. In fact, Disney's first business in which he created original cartoons, which were one-minute reel cartoons called Laugh-O-Grams, was devised in that garage. Walt had been making several short films depicting current events in a satirical manner, like the February 1921 Kansas City police department reorganization, the delays in the city streetcar service, the horrible conditions of the pothole-riddled roads of the city, trends in crime, and women's fashion. He also made lightning sketch style animations using himself, including a lightning sketch introduction to one of his animated cartoons. He named these cartoons, which he punched into a 200-foot single running cartoon, "Local Happenings." He showed some of these to his former boss and then-friend Louis Pesmen, who advised Walt to show them to one of his clients, Frank Newman, who was in the movie theater business. As always, in order to catch Newman's eye, he named them Newman's Laugh-O-Grams, without even asking the man. According to Elias Disney, Newman was the "big showman in Kansas City at that time." He had three movie theaters in Kansas City, the last one being The Newman, which had opened in June 1919. It was the manager of this theater, Milton

Herbert Feld, who actually went on to become a Hollywood producer, that Disney went to with his Laugh-O-Grams, although his own accounts vary as to who he actually dealt with, Newman or Feld.

Whatever the case, one thing is certain—his Laugh-O-Grams were not only bought, but he was also asked to make more. When Walt went to the theater in hopes of selling his reels as a regular feature, Newman or Feld, whoever was actually there, was impressed by his work. Not only did they want to buy all of them, but they also wanted Walt to make one every week. Walt later remembered that he was so taken over by excitement that, when asked if they would be costly to make, he just quoted the price of thirty cents per foot off the top of his head, selling the existing reel at sixty dollars. It was only after the deal had been made, about an hour after Walt left the theater office, that he realized his mistake—he had agreed to sell them at cost price and had forgotten to add any profit. But Walt was thankful to at least be getting such a great opportunity for exposure.

Walt's Laugh-O-Grams debuted in the theater on March 20th, 1921, when Walt was just nineteen. The program schedule at The Newman frequently featured a section called Newman News and Views, a compilation of shorts on world events edited by the management staff of the top film weeklies, as well as of local news captured by the Newman staff cameraman. Thus, Walt's work fit in perfectly with this section. It was mentioned in the *Kansas City Star* and was well received by audiences. Besides Laugh-O-Grams, Walt often did other work for Newman, too, although none of it was actually profitable. Feld would often ask him to animate movie stars, current political scenarios, and even holidays. During this time, Walt also created Dr. Whosis, his first named cartoon character that punished rowdy movie patrons. Walt saw the situation as someone paying money for his experimental work while also providing free exposure, which was a win-win situation for him. Cauger was proud to have an employee that had some local fame, and he often showed Walt and his work off at various places or to try to bring in new clients, although he himself was very reluctant to adopt Disney's new methods for his own company.

Although Disney's pay was meager for his work at Newman's, he still had to run after Gus Eyssell, Newman's treasurer, for his pay. In spite of that, Walt was earning a decent amount. His starting salary at the Kansas City Film Ad Company had risen from forty dollars to sixty dollars a week by now, after about eighteen months of working there. Walt had made significant savings by then and decided to strike out on his own once more. But now, wizened up by his past experiences, he decided to keep this job as a back-up. This was a clever move, as his brother Herbert, who worked as a mail carrier, and his family were moving to Portland, Oregon, and Walt's parents would follow on November 6th, 1921. While it is not known for sure if they sold their Kansas City house, Walt bought his own studio at around the very same time, which indicates that he probably no longer had access to the garage. He got a small space above a streetcar barn and opened the studio with Fred Harman, a young colleague from the Film Ad Company and who is best known today for the *Red Ryder* comic strip. They were inspired by Paul Terry, whose *Aesop's Fables* were gaining prominence since June that year, to make it big with this studio and then leave the Film Ad Company. The two used their savings from their job to buy a second-hand Universal movie camera and a tripod for $300. Their plan was to make a good film and use that both for income as well as promotion for their studio to bring in more clients. Fred had a younger brother, Hugh, who was still in his junior year at Westport High School and who was highly attracted to the studio. Hugh would often run to the studio after school was over in the afternoon and stayed all evening to assist with the animation work, even though it hampered his studies.

The first cartoon in question was called "The Little Artist," in which the artist drew a character that came to life on his easel and had a conversation with him. This took months to create because both men had their day jobs. They would work all day at the Film Ad

Company, have a quick meal, and then work all night at the studio. Hugh actually thought that they hardly seemed to sleep, possibly because they were in a hurry to complete the work on which their future hinged. It is interesting to note that Walt probably did not have his own living quarters either because when Fred and Walt did find the time to sleep, Walt would go with Fred to the Elsmere Hotel, where the Harmans, including Fred, Hugh, and a third brother named Walker, lived with another roommate. In the meantime, they also shot some live-action films and unsuccessfully tried to convince a local daily, the *Kansas City Journal*, to collaborate on a newsreel segment for some extra money.

About this time, the two young men formally named their studio Kaycee Studios, a stylized version of KC, or Kansas City, where they were based. They had probably used a rudimentary name like Harman-Disney Studios to start with, though. They also played with various special effects, like reverse footage, where Walt shot a live-action scene and then played it backward, as well as multiple roles, where the same person was seen as more than one character in the same scene. Walt had tried the former with his niece and his mother while they were still in the city. For the latter, he had used himself as the model. By this time, they had moved the studio to above the storefront office of the Standard Phonograph Company at 3241 Troost Avenue, with there probably being another intermediary location.

Walt and Fred were still employed with Cauger during this time. Walt had even been trying to get Cauger to try out the new methods they had been experimenting with, but he failed to change Cauger's mind, and anyway, Cauger had deals in place with many companies for his slide films. So, Walt and Fred tried to compete not only with Cauger but also with the other local ad film companies for assignments at local theaters. They used their savings to buy a second-hand Model T Ford coupe to go around the city and meet up with managers of film theaters to try and sell them their work. They even drove to neighboring cities and towns of Kansas and Missouri to try to sign deals with the theaters there. But they steered clear of the theaters that Cauger was selling to. Despite this, Cauger did not take this too kindly, seeing them as competitors who also happened to be his employees. Cauger may have even gone so far as to take away the camera he had lent to Walt, forcing them to rely only on the Universal one. At one point, they drove to Atherton in Missouri to shoot a film in sepia known as "The Old Mill," in which another special effect was used by Disney whereby a drawing of an old man beside a mill transitioned into a live-action scene. Unfortunately for them, they did not succeed much in these attempts and started to struggle financially. They were unable to pay their rent, and the car was repossessed too.

However, not too long after the studio started, the duo finally scored big. The American Legion Convention was being organized at Kansas City, from October 30th to November 1st, 1921. Kaycee Studios had landed the assignment of covering the event for the French newsreel and documentary production company Pathé News. The pay was fantastic—a dollar per foot of good quality, usable film, which meant Kaycee Studios stood to make a profit of 95 cents per foot of filmed reel, or 1,900 percent. But there was one catch: the film had to be an aerial view of the event, which meant Walt and Fred would have to shoot from a plane. They had never even been on a plane before, let alone shoot from one. But they did not want to pass up such a lucrative opportunity, one that would allow them to get rid of their financial struggles. So, they set out to do it anyway.

At first, they had decided that they would fly in two different planes so they could get more footage from different angles. The night before the job, they sneaked into the Kansas City Film Ad Company office basement to "borrow" one of Cauger's cameras. But on the actual day, October 30th, after a test flight without a camera, an idea that had been suggested by the pilot of one of the two World War I Flying Jennys they were to fly in, Fred decided they should fly together. He said that flying alone and trying to handle a camera while keeping oneself stable in the plane would be too risky.

Moreover, if they broke Cauger's camera, they would be in huge trouble. So, they decided to use their own Universal camera, with Fred holding the tripod in place and Walt cranking it. They returned Cauger's camera back to its place the very next day.

The duo was supposed to capture the stunt flying of the airplanes participating in the aerial show of the convention from their plane. On November 1st, there was a parade in Kansas City held by the Legion members. Walt and Fred had hauled their camera and equipment to the roof of a building owned by the father of a school friend of Walt's, which was located opposite the reviewing stand of the parade. This optimum position allowed them to capture both the parade and the dignitaries reviewing it. Afterward, the two sent the reels for development with great hopes of fabulous footage and good money from Pathé News. But their hopes were dashed regarding the air show. A cameraman friend had advised them, in regards to the aerial shooting, to keep the exposure at a minimum to prevent too much backlight from darkening the subject. But either the advice was faulty or Walt and Fred had misunderstood the instructions because everything came out dark. With that, their dream of quick money and better days at Kaycee was shattered.

The frustration of their struggling business would ultimately get to them in the following weeks. Walt brought in another colleague from the Film Ad Company to help them at Kaycee. William McAtee Lyon, also known as Red Lyon, was good with the camera, and so, Walt brought him in as a partner. This did not go down well with Fred, though, because he felt like Walt was further dividing up an already dwindling asset. It may also have had something to do with the fact that Red claimed to be a Hollywood veteran, and Walt gave him a lot of importance because of that. So, around November or December, Fred left but not on a bitter note. The two remained on good terms and often exchanged correspondence. The "air flight" incident was just one of the anecdotes that Fred would recount humorously to friends later on in life. Walt kept working for Pathé News, along with Red, as a correspondent for them in Kansas City in case Pathé needed any news or events covered there. The pay was good, as it was at a dollar per foot for 100 feet, which would be replaced in case Pathé did not accept the film. But the work was errant, and Walt wanted to return to cartooning, his first love.

For this, Walt decided to make short, one-reel fairy tales, setting them in modern times to give them a humorous twist. He picked Little Red Riding Hood as his first project and devoted his nights and any extra time he had after his day job and Pathé to making this cartoon film. About this time, either at the end of 1921 or at the beginning of 1922, the Standard Phonograph Company was replaced by a café called Peiser's Restaurant, owned by the German Rudolph Peiser. As the new year rolled in, Walt realized what a strenuous and exhausting job animation was, especially now that he was the only one actually doing it. He knew he needed extra hands on deck, but he also knew that he couldn't offer anyone a salary. So, he instead employed some diplomatic methods to not only get the assistance he needed but also not have to pay for it. The answer was an unpaid internship. Walt put out an advertisement in the classifieds of the *Kansas City Star* under the "Education" section, asking for art students and aspiring artists who wanted a hands-on learning experience in "motion picture cartooning" on February 5th. But due to the poor response, he was forced to publish another advertisement on March 8th, this time in the "Help Wanted" section, looking for a cartoonist for "motion picture work."

In all probability, Rudolf "Rudy" Carl Ising, a bright young eighteen-year-old with a curiosity to learn animation, was the only one that responded and joined, although Walt said there were others. For as long as he remembered, he and Walt had been the only ones in the studio since Red had left Kaycee soon after Rudy joined, which was early 1922. Hugh and Ub came by at times, and that was pretty much it. Rudy had left a four-year-long job with the E.H. Roberts Portrait Company to join a cartooning course in London and was not bothered about the initial lack of pay Walt offered him. He described the studio as a frugal "50 x 200" space, with a few desks partitioned into workspaces and offices by cardboard because they did not have the money for plywood, a fact corroborated by Hugh Harman. Rudy also noted that Walt's skills were quite basic; clearly, the book by Lutz was his only source of knowledge, which meant that the learning part that had drawn Rudy to the job in the first place did not pan out as he had hoped. But he got to work in animating cartoons, and that was enough for the time being.

Besides the Red Riding Hood film, Rudy was also assisting Walt in making a series of 300-foot shorts using cartoons and sarcastic jokes to talk about current hot topics. They were called the "Lafflets." They often used the lightning sketch technique, cel animation, and claymation, and around three of them were completed by May of that year. *Little Red Riding Hood* was completed even earlier, around the beginning of spring that year, and stood at six minutes and seventeen seconds. It had six animated characters in total, four of which would become recurring characters in subsequent works. Rudy had worked as the camera operator on *Little Red Riding Hood*. But he finally got to animate, as he had originally wanted, when Walt asked him to animate *The Four Musicians of Bremen*, his next film. They finished this sometime around May that year. However, Walt went deeper and deeper into debt. Rudy recounted how, at one point, a process server kept calling at their office to serve a notice for outstanding bills to "Mr. Walt Dinsey," and Walt himself would keep saying that Mr. Dinsey was not in. He was only caught one day because his childhood friend, Walter Pfeiffer, had come to visit, and he accidentally called Walt by name just as the server was entering. Rudy felt bad for him and helped Walt with a 500-dollar loan out of the $1,000 he had saved while working at the E.H. Roberts Portrait Company. Yet, it was surprising how Walt felt quite confident in his abilities and skills. He thought that he had enough experience in cartooning, animation, and films to be able to start his own truly standalone cartoon animation studio. This time, he decided to quit his Kansas City Film Ad Company job for good.

# Chapter 4: New Leaf

In May 1922, Walt incorporated his new Laugh-O-Gram Studio to make a series of fairy tales set in the modern world, just like *Little Red Riding Hood*. The stocks were divided into 300 shares at a value of $50 each. Fifty-one percent of these stocks were ascribed to the corporation itself, which gave the company assets of $7,752. Of this, $2,700 was raised from investors as cash, while $5,052 was in the form of physical assets. This consisted of his short *The Four Musicians of Bremen* and the "Lafflets," which were valued at $3,000, and the rest of the $2,052 was comprised of the furniture and animation equipment used back at Kaycee. Walt himself was the largest shareholder, with seventy shares to his name, while some of the significant investors he lured onto the project were father and son William and Fletcher Hammond, Red Lyon, and Edmund J. Wolf, presented in order of ownership size. Thus, on May 18$^{th}$, Walt signed the articles of association, with himself as the president, and Lyon, the Hammonds, and Wolf signed on the Board of Directors. It is difficult to say how much of this was legal since Walt was still twenty and thus a minor. In spite of this, the articles were recorded on May 19$^{th}$, and a recorder's certificate was issued the following day. On May 23rd, Laugh-O-Gram Films, Inc. finally received its certificate of incorporation from the state of Missouri.

Walt finished setting up the studio on May 28th on the second floor of the McConahy Building. The suite had five rooms—the two in the south were the animating room and the laboratory and camera room, while the three in the north were the lobby and an office partitioned off into spaces for Walt's drawing board, the office manager, and a secretary. Soon, on May 28th and 29th, Walt put out ads in the *Kansas City Star*, looking for cartoonists and animators, "experienced or inexperienced." It was almost comical that Walt, who himself had hardly any formal training in animation, was confident that he could groom any inexperienced person that joined. Walt, Red, and Rudy, who were the only ones with any background at all, went on to hire five men who responded to the ad. There was Lorey Tague, hired as an animator, Carmen "Max" Maxwell, also hired as an animator for ten dollars per week, Alexander Wilson Kurfiss, hired as an artist who also made posters there, and Otto Louis Walliman, who did the backgrounds in the animation drawings. Besides these, there were two other people that Walt hired, whom he already knew very well.

The first was Hugh Harman, who was nineteen at the time and came to know of Walt's new studio from Fred. Hugh had just completed his officer's training at Fort Riley and had an appointment for cavalry school in West Point. Out of curiosity, though, he decided to check out the office, and Walt convinced him to stay and work with him. He was paid 25 dollars a week. His experience only included some high school yearbook drawings and his time spent at the Kaycee Studios when his elder brother worked there. Besides him, there was Walt's childhood buddy, Walter Pfeiffer, who worked there in the capacity of a scenario editor, which simply meant that he was supposed to scan print materials for jokes and incorporate them into the scenarios of the cartoon. He was a Westport High School graduate, just like Hugh, and was the same age as him as well, and he had done drawings for the annual yearbook of his school.

Other than these, there was Adolph "Jack" Kloepper, who was hired by Walt as a business manager for fifty dollars a week. Leslie Mace, the ex-husband of Esther Ida Hammond, who was the daughter of William Hammond, had worked before as a salesman, and so, Walt hired him as a general sales manager, tasked with procuring a distribution contract in light of a June 1922 article in the *Motion Picture News*. It said that he had been making films for the Newman Theatre for the past couple years and that he had six films ready that he intended to release every two weeks. This was obviously not true and was only a publicity gimmick to attract distributors. When it failed, Walt published another article in the papers in July that twelve Laugh-O-Grams were ready and waiting for a distributor, which was an even bigger lie, since besides *Little Red Riding Hood* and *The Four Musicians of Bremen*, Walt had only gotten *Jack and the Beanstalk* finished by August. Walt sent Mace to New York in August for a month, along with Dr. John Vance Cowles, Sr., an eminent Kansas City physician with clients like Harry Truman, who would one day be the president of the United States. He had come on the team of Laugh-O-Gram Studio as the treasurer of the company and probably became an investor, too. Walt had met him while photographing the children of Dr. Cowles—Minnie Jeanett Cowles, John V. Cowles Jr, and Virginia Cowles—on Minnie's birthday sometime in the summer of 1922, probably as a favor.[1]

The two went to New York with the express purpose of finding a distributor, but Mace failed miserably. Worse, he spent a lot of money staying in the McAlpine Hotel. Disney, quite strictly, ordered him back to Kansas City, but Mace did not want to return empty-handed, so he struck a hasty deal with William Kelley, the Tennessee representative of Pictorial Clubs, Inc., a non-commercial entity that distributed films to schools and churches, on September 16th, 1922. However, the deal had red flags all over it. It said that Disney would make them six Laugh-O-Gram fairy tales. They

---

[1] http://msonntag.blogspot.com/2011/08/walt-in-kansas-1922-rediscovered.html

bought the rights to the cartoons by signing a contract for a down payment of only $100. They also stipulated that they would only pay the rest of the money, which was $11,000, on January 1st, 1924, i.e., fifteen months later, and only upon completion of the films. The terms of the deal were preposterous, as animation was a capital-intensive process, and not getting a regular supply of funds throughout the process would obviously make the company run into serious financial trouble. Mace knew this very well, so he quit the studio as soon as he returned to Kansas City, which was around the middle of October.

But Walt decided not to be cowed by this setback. With renewed vigor, he started working on his cartoons. With his beefed-up staff, he was completing the work in record time. *The Four Musicians of Bremen* and *Little Red Riding Hood* were already completed, and he made four more by October. These were *Puss in Boots*, *Goldie Locks and the Three Bears*, *Jack and the Beanstalk*, and *Jack the Giant Killer*. As the work progressed, the members of Walt's team also became more experienced. This became apparent in the fact that they tackled more and more complex and detailed scenes in the latter cartoons. But it was also obvious that their finances were dwindling because the methods and resources used became simpler and "primitive." He was also trying to commercialize baby photoshoots of the kind he had done for Dr. Cowles' children.

Walt also decided to add more employees to the company, without considering the payroll burden he would be adding to the finances that were already chipping away fast, almost to the tune of "about four hundred more each week," as Red had written in a letter to his mother around the middle of October. The most significant addition had been Ub Iwerks, Walt's first business partner. There had probably been some talk of Ub joining the studio before, but it is not known whether Walt had asked him or if Ub had finally shown interest. Ub had decided against it back then due to the fact that he required a steady salary from his job at the Kansas City Film Ad Company to support his mother and that Walt's enterprise was riddled with doubts of success. In a way, Ub's qualms had not been ill-founded since the company would run into debt soon. But, for whatever reason, sometime in November of 1922, he decided to quit the Film Ad Company and join the Laugh-O-Gram Studio as a letterer. However, Ub's innovative streak, which had become apparent even when he was working at the Film Ad Company, where he had made an automated system of cranking the camera for smoother and less jaunty movements, was working wonders here, too. He taught the rest of them how to automatically enlarge or reduce the animation drawings, using a device he invented that would later come to be called the "biff-sniff."

Another addition to the team was Nadine Simpson. She was a 26-year-old who worked at the local Film Exchange and had once dated Rudy Ising. She would use her connections to procure reels too worn out for use and give them to the group to study. Simpson had once allowed the group to discreetly borrow one of Paul Terry's cartoons from *Aesop's Fables*, more specifically, the one of Farmer Al Falfa. It greatly helped the group as they learned about cycles that were used to depict repetitive action by running a small strip continuously. In November of that year, Disney hired Nadine as a bookkeeper and stenographer for the studio. He also brought in 21-old Aletha Reynolds as an inker, painter, and editor for the "Lafflets" at twelve dollars a week. However, even as the studio finished making the last of the Laugh-O-Grams for Pictorial Clubs, which was *Cinderella*, they were "down to the last penny." Walt had no choice but to turn to his treasurer John Cowles for help. John, being their treasurer as well as an investor, must have been reluctant to loan to a company that hardly had much hope of revival, but having a personal stake in it, he lent $2,500 to Walt anyway on Thanksgiving Day, 1922. Walt promised to pay him back within ninety days with six percent interest. It is safe to speculate that Walt was quite unsuccessful in doing so since his balance was running in the negative. This was only the first of many small loans that would tide the studio over until the spring of 1923.

During this time, a much-needed relief came in the form of Dr. Thomas McCrum, a 46-year-old local dentist. He asked Walt to make an educational children's film on the benefits of dental hygiene. Dr. McCrum had visited the studio office the first time to discuss the project. The next time, when he asked Walt to come down to see him and take the money, Walt said he couldn't—he had given his only pair of shoes for repair, and the cobbler would not give it back unless Walt gave him the $1.50 he owed for it. So, Dr. McCrum not only came over and gave the $1.50 to get back Walt's shoes, but he also gave them $500 to start production, which happened right away. The film was to be called *Tommy Tucker's Tooth*.

Walt, along with Rudy and Dr. McCrum, went to Benton Grammar School, which was the alma mater of Disney and Pfeiffer, to scout for actors and a location. Dr. McCrum, being a respected man, was granted permission by the principal of the school to have his film shot there using one of their own boys. The teachers of the school even selected a few candidates that they thought would be suitable and showed them to the team. An eleven-year-old sixth grader by the name of John "Jack" Records was finally selected to play the role of Jimmie Jones in the film. The story is that Jimmie Jones is a boy who does not at all care for his dental hygiene because he considers it to be too girly, while Tommy Tucker has perfectly healthy teeth. As a result, when they are both interviewed for the same job, Tommy is chosen due to his cleaner looks over Jimmie. This prompts Jimmie to go see a dentist, and subsequently, he gets a job at the same place as well. The whole thing is narrated by a woman who teaches children why dental health is so important, and the film ends with a guide on the proper way to brush one's teeth. Although the initial plan was for a live-action film, which it did mostly turn out to be, Walt felt it would be nice to add a few animations to show a cartoon version of how things work inside the mouth. That December was spent by Disney and Pfeiffer in the school, as they shot the live-action scenes, while Rudy spent that time in the studio working on the animations. The finished product was a 10-minute 34-second long film. Walt even invited Jack Records to check out their office and gave him a small reward of five or ten dollars for his acting. He had paid similar amounts to the other kids he had hired from the school, too. Funnily enough, Jack's future fiancée would see the film in a home nursing class. Walt himself got only about fifty to sixty dollars out of the venture.

# Chapter 5: Brush with Bankruptcy

The winter of 1922-23 was a very dark and trying time for the studio, as well as for Walt. Walt had been unable to pay many of his staff their due salary for a few weeks now, and they were leaving one by one. This included Pfeiffer, who moved to Chicago and to whom he already owed $96.50, as well as Lorey Tague, who had not been paid for some time in December. Red Lyon had also moved to California. Walt was in debt to several suppliers of the studio, and along with some of the other staff, he had run up a credit at the Forest Inn Café, a place on the first floor of the McConahy Building, whose owners Jerry Raggos and Louis Katsos, felt bad for the boys who were just scraping by. But Walt remembered later in life that even they stopped being so kind after some time, giving them the cheapest, lowest quality food and leftovers, and that when his debt went over sixty dollars, they stopped keeping a credit line for him. During this time, Nadine Simpson, the company's secretary, often fed Walt and the boys so that they would not starve. Yet that was not possible all the time, and Walt often made his meals out of bread and beans directly from the can.

When the owners of the Forest Inn Café caught Walt going through the garbage cans for food, they let him eat at the café on credit again.

Walt also started sleeping on the studio floor more often because he did not have the money to pay the three-dollar monthly rent to his landlady or to any other boarding house. He used to use the restroom at the end of the McConahy Building and walked to the Union Station once a week for a shower that cost a dime. During this time, he only managed to scrape by due to help from Roy. Roy was diagnosed with tuberculosis back in 1920 and had been bouncing around from one sanatorium to the other, starting with one in Santa Fe in New Mexico, then one in Arizona, and finally landed in the Veterans Hospital in Sawtelle, California. Roy would, from time to time, send Walt a blank check that Walt was allowed to fill with any amount up to thirty dollars, which would come from Roy's disability checks for his navy service. Walt was so cash-strapped that he always wrote for the full thirty dollars. He would also often end up in the house of Edna Francis, who was Roy's girlfriend, hungry and kind of delusional, and she would give him his first square meal in days.

Then, on January 4th, 1923, E.M. McConahy, the owner of the McConahy Building, sued Disney and the Laugh-O-Gram Studio for an overhead of $384 gathered in rent. The studio avoided eviction due to another loan from Dr. John Cowles. W.J. Cairns, the justice of the peace, directed Walt and the studio to repay the outstanding fee, along with $12.90 as interest and legal expenses. In February, John Schmeltz, a German hardware store owner on their Board of Directors, wrote Walt a check for $482.51 for their outstanding bill at the Briggs Supply Co. for lamps they had bought from them, against a chattel mortgage totaling $506.76, with three Perkins Hi-Power lamp moving picture machines with stands and a Cooper-Hewitt tube as collateral, with six percent interest payable within six months.

Walt also started working on a revamped version of the "Lafflets" during this time. In fact, many of the "Lafflets" had been redone to create some of these shorts. They were mostly worked on by Aletha Reynolds, Rudy Ising, and Ub Iwerks. Some of these included

"Aesthetic Camping," "A Pirate for a Day," "A Star Pitcher," "The Woodland Potter." Jack Kloepper sent a few of these samples to Universal Studios with the proposition of a business deal, assuring them they would soon go into distribution. In fact, Walt had been talking to a distributor, Inter-Ocean, in early February, and besides Universal, he had also had Commercial Traders Cinema Corporation in mind. But even though they had shown some interest, the project was soon scrapped since no distribution deal had materialized. With impending doom on their heads, the principal shareholders, Walt, Rudy, and Cowles, decided to have a stockholder meeting for the recapitalization of the shares of the company on March 17th. Their cumulative value was raised from $15,000 to $50,000, with the issuance of 1,000 shares, of which 350 would be owned by Walt and 350 by Cowles. The whole process was completed and approved much later in July, but by that time, it was too late.

March of 1923 was quite an eventful month for Walt besides this meeting. Walt often used to visit the Isis Theater, and this turned out to be a major turning point in Walt's life because this was where he cultivated a friendship with Carl Stalling, who would not only give him a new job but also go on to play a leading role in providing music to many of Disney's iconic works later on. Carl was the organist at the Isis Theater, where he usually accompanied the silent films with music from his piano. Carl was an alumnus of Kansas City Conservatory of Music, and he started as an organist at the theater, soon becoming its music director. He and Walt already knew each other somewhat from when some of Walt's Laugh-O-Grams used to play at the theater. This time, Carl asked Walt to make a sing-along film to go with the song "Martha: Just a Plain Old Fashioned Name." Walt called it a Sing-O-Reel, but basically, it was a lyrical music video. The film ran for some time at the theater but soon went out.

Coinciding with this was the start of the production of *Alice's Wonderland*, the most ambitious project of Laugh-O-Gram Studio yet. The inspiration for this came from the *Out of the Inkwell* series made by Max and Dave Fleischer, where Koko the Clown climbs out of the artist's inkpot, thus putting an animated character in a live-action world. Walt planned to do the opposite with *Alice's Wonderland*, putting the live-action character Alice in an animated world, hoping to cash in on some of the popularity that the *Inkwell* series enjoyed. He even started the production of a sample pilot episode in March. As he did, he also started looking for a suitable child actor for the role of Alice. Walt probably first spotted Virginia Davis in a Kansas City Film Ad Company ad at the theater, as it came out around the same time he was scouting, and decided that this four-year-old girl would be perfect for the role. After some negotiations, a contract was finally drawn between Walt and the Davises on April 13th, where Virginia would receive five percent of the profits that the cartoon would make. Perhaps this was a clever move by Walt so that he would not be under the obligation to pay a fixed salary to the actor from the already drained treasury of the studio. But they still needed money for expenses, and once again, Schmeltz cut them another check.

It is interesting to note that Dr. Cowles had, by then, stopped helping Walt or the company financially. This was probably due to the fact that it had become known during this time that the Tennessee unit of Pictorial had gone bankrupt and had been absorbed into the main New York unit, making it impossible for them to pay the 11,000 they owed the studio. Realizing there was no way to salvage the company, it is likely that the already skeptical Dr. Cowles had entirely withdrawn himself from making any more offers of financial help. But Walt truly believed he was about to strike gold with *Alice's Wonderland* and kept moving forward with the shooting and animation. He planned to make full-length reels to be released monthly and bi-monthly. The cartoon was initially supposed to be called *Alice in Cartoonland*, due to the fact that the story involved Alice traveling to an animated land called Cartoonland, but for some reason, it was renamed.

The working title was *Alice in Slumberland* since the animated part happens in a dream sequence. The story goes that Alice went to visit the Laugh-O-Gram Studio, where she sees the characters drawn by the animators, played by Walt, Ub, Rudy, and Hugh, come to life, leaving the canvas and frolicking around the room. That night, she dreams of taking a train to the magical land of Cartoonland, where she is greeted by all the animals in a great parade. She rides atop an animated elephant to go from the station and then goes to a party of the animated animals where they do a dance for each other. But the party is interrupted by lions that have escaped from the Cartoonland zoo. The lions chase her, first into a hollow tree, then a cave, then down a rabbit hole, and finally to a cliff. She wakes up when she jumps from the cliff.

The live-action parts were filmed in Virginia's own house and the Laugh-O-Gram studio. The scenes in the animated world were created by making Virginia act in front of a whiteboard based on instructions given by Walt and leaving space for the cartoon characters and background, which would be added later in the normal animation process, a method once again thought up by Ub. Most of the actual animation was said to have been done by Hugh, and it continued well into May. By this time, a lot of the staff working in the studio had left. For example, Aletha, quit the job on April 8th, seeing no chance of getting paid. Nadine, who was owed an indefinite amount, not only in back pay but also the innumerable times she helped the team out with money, also left on May 1st. Perhaps the biggest blow came when Ub left on May 5th to resume his job at the Film Ad Company after over 1,000 dollars had been accumulated in debt payable to him. They all stayed on as long as they could, though, and only left when they could no longer make do without money.

In his desperate search for a distributor, Walt wrote to Margaret J. Winkler, the original distributor for the *Out of the Inkwell* cartoons. Margaret Winkler was quite a notable figure in the animation scene at that time. She was the first female producer and distributor of animated films and was also the only one at that time. She had started out as the personal secretary of Harry Warner, co-founder of Warner Brothers. Seeing her talent and skill, Harry encouraged her to form her own distribution company and take on the Fleischer brothers as her first clients for the *Out of the Inkwell* cartoons when she showed interest in the series. She was also the force behind Pat Sullivan's Felix the Cat cartoons. Now, Winkler's company, M.J. Winkler Productions, was also seeing the possibility of an impending crisis of going out of business and became very interested in Walt's proposition in May. But production was not complete, and on top of that, besides owing Rudy for his work, he also owed money to Clifford Collingsworth, who had taken over the lease from McConahy. Collingsworth was way less forgiving than McConahy. Sometime in the first half of May, he decided to hold the studio and all their equipment and materials hostage until at least some of the accumulated rent was paid back.

This forced them to turn again to Schmeltz for assistance, but he was adamant. He did not want to risk his money unless it was against some sort of security. He asked for a second chattel mortgage for six percent interest against Laugh-O-Gram property and also the Pictorial assignment. Unfortunately, the studio was going through such difficult times that said property ended up being all of the office furniture and technical equipment, including even the coat rack and four wastebaskets.

Accordingly, on May 19th, Schmeltz forwarded 750 dollars to the studio's bank account and guaranteed the payment of the outstanding rent to Collingsworth. He also agreed to help Walt pay back some of the staff and people he owed. Collingsworth allowed Walt and his people back on the premises, but he had to vacate the suite as soon as possible. Seeing no other choice, Walt struck a deal with Rudolph Peiser so he could occupy the room above Peiser's restaurant again, signing the lease on May 24th, 1923. After they settled in, they resumed work on *Alice's Wonderland*. Finally, on June 18th, Walt was able to reply to Margaret, but it was not a hopeful letter. He apologized for the delay and informed her that due to certain "delays and setbacks" pertaining to the shift of base, he would be unable to deliver the *Alice* cartoons in June but would be able to see her on July 1st in New York with the sample to discuss future plans. Winkler, enthusiastic, replied within a week, saying she was looking forward to it, but unfortunately, this time, too, it did not materialize. This was due to the studio being financially crippled, understaffed, and another unforeseen event that almost undid all their hard work.

On the financial side, on June 22nd, Walt, Rudy Ising, and Dr. Cowles made the move of signing, and thus, approving the "Statement of Increase of Capital Stock" they had been sitting on since March. Rudy left the very next day, with Walt owing him 711.23 dollars. It was down to only Walt Disney and Hugh Harman now. The final shock came in the form of the discovery that part of the *Alice* negatives had melted in the summer heat; they had to reshoot those parts all over again. All of this meant that *Alice's Wonderland* was far from ready when Margaret had last written to him about it. When it was completed, it was 12 minutes and 25 seconds. But some things were yet to be done, and Walt was still unable to take Margaret Winkler up on her deal.

It was clear by July, even to a person like Walt, who was driven and optimistic to a fault, that there was no longer any hope for Laugh-O-Gram Studio—it was, beyond a doubt, on its last breath. Jack Kloepper, who still had to be paid $499 of the $547 owed to him, quit on July 6th and immediately proceeded to move to court for it. Schmeltz also had to pay the $75 rent to Peiser for Walt since he had a major stake in the studio now. One last straw Walt had been clutching at was a deal with the *Kansas City Post* to make a weekly newsreel for them, which had been a nebulous idea he had had with Fred Harman in the early days of Kaycee Studios. When that also produced nothing, Walt utterly and thoroughly knew it was over. He started considering going to work for another studio, perhaps in New York, which was a big deal because Walt's entrepreneurial desires had always been so strong that he had started to work independently even while in the Kansas City Film Ad Company. To want to abandon the dream of owning his own studio indicated that Walt no longer believed in his abilities. Roy also advised him to leave Kansas City, as that was not the place to be an animator. But Roy, instead of telling him to go to New York, which was where the animation scene was the biggest, told him to go to Los Angeles, California, since their uncle Robert lived there.

Walt agreed to this advice, even if it meant he had to pursue a career in live-action movies from then on. However, he did not even have money for a ticket to California. So, he did the one thing he knew best—he earned for it. With the little amount of money he had left, presumably from the meager proceeds from *Martha*, he bought a movie camera that he claimed was "antiquated" and went from door to door in an affluent residential neighborhood in the city, offering to shoot pictures and videos of babies for between ten to fifteen dollars. The only names that Walt remembered from this stint were that of his first customers, Dr. Leland Viley and his wife. He shot 200 feet of footage of their six-month-old baby Kathalee, lovingly called Kay. Soon, others followed, and when Walt had made enough for a ticket, he sold the camera to a movie enthusiast for double the cost, using the aforementioned "antiquated" status to make a profitable sale, which gave him a bit of extra money for the journey. He bought a first-class ticket in the Santa Fe, California Limited, the same train that used to run through Marceline. The exact date of his departure is not reliably known because he claimed to have never really informed anyone who could give a reliable account later on. He just packed up and left, with only an old suit, a sweater, some of his drawing materials, and the *Alice* cartoon in a cheap, leather-finish pasteboard suitcase.

Walt did have dinner the night before in the house of Edna Francis, Roy's girlfriend, and was given food for the journey by Herbert's mother-in-law and dropped at the station by her son. While Walt had always insisted that nobody came to see him off, a lot of people begged to differ, including Rudy, Ub, and Edna. He had not even cleared out the studio space above Peiser's or appeared for the hearing for Kloepper's unpaid debt. As a result, the court ruled in favor of Kloepper, directing Laugh-O-Gram Studio to pay him back with fourteen dollars interest. Of course, there was nobody there at the moment because even Hugh had gotten a job at the Kansas City Film Ad Company on the recommendation of Walt. Meanwhile, Schmeltz had forwarded $367.61 more to Collingsworth, as well as two checks to the Laugh-O-Gram account, probably unaware that there was nobody left to help out.

# Chapter 6: Hello to Hollywood

Roy received a 21-year-old Walt, who was dressed in a mismatched coat and pants, at LA on a warm California August day of 1923. Of course, he could not stay with Roy—Roy was still recuperating in Sawtelle's Veterans Hospital. So, Walt put up in his uncle Robert's house. Robert lived there with his wife, Charlotte, and his German Shepherd dog, Peggy. Walt paid a weekly $5 rent, which came from Roy's disability allowance of $65.

At this time, Walt, freshly disenchanted with the idea of cartooning, which had gotten him nowhere, thought his best course of action would be to go into motion pictures. He wished to become a director, but he was up for any job that any studio would give him at that point. He felt that once he got a job, he could study the film business up close and would slowly build his way up to the higher ranks. But Walt was not being exactly honest when he said that. The truth was that he might have been looking for some odd jobs here and there, but in reality, he still wanted to have his own business. Walt started frequenting studios just to see how things worked. One of his biggest ruses was getting into studios and sets by saying he was looking for a job. In this way, he successfully managed to get onto the lots of Paramount Studio and Vitagraph Studios, among others. But the two places he used to haunt the most were Universal Studios and Metro-Goldwyn Mayer (MGM) Studios. One of his friends from Kansas City working in Paramount had even gotten him the part of an extra in the film *The Light That Failed* as a cavalryman, but he lost it to unfortunate circumstances. All in all, no matter in what capacity Walt tried to get a job, he was turned away.

But as much as Walt claimed that he was done with cartoons, he had really not given up. He kept meeting up with distributors, showing them *Alice's Wonderland* and even "Mr. George's Wife," a comic strip he made in 1920 but never published, but he could get no one interested. Basically, everyone told him to try in New York, which was the animation capital of the US back then, just like Hollywood was the motion picture capital. Thankfully, Walt decided to call upon Margaret Winkler once again to see if she might still be interested. He wrote to her on August 25$^{th}$, with a printed letterhead showing "Walt Disney, Cartoonist" and the address being given as his uncle's, saying that he was no longer associated with his old studio and was setting up a new one in LA. He laid out his necessity to have a "working space" in an established "studio," where he could not only be acquainted with better equipment, methods, and content in the form of "technical detail and comedy situations" but where he could also be able to hire experienced actors and staff for producing the films. He attributed his earlier failure to deliver to a lack of the above. However, Walt did express the desire to bring in a few of his earlier staff, probably because he felt a level of comfort and compatibility with them, and said that if these conditions could be arranged, he could start producing on a regular basis. To be on the safe side, he wrote to her that due to the aforementioned obstacles, *Alice's Wonderland* was not on par with the level of quality he envisioned and that he could make it right with the right facilities and hands.

Either by luck or coincidence, Margaret Winkler was actually going through desperate times and was on the lookout for a new cartoon to endorse. She was on the verge of losing the rights to the *Out of the*

*Inkwell* series due to the Fleischers starting Fleischer Studios. On top of that, she also feared that the immense popularity of the *Felix the Cat* series would lead to its creator, Pat Sullivan, trying to leverage impossible demands in the new contract that would be drawn up after the current one expired, which was very soon. In fact, just a week prior to Margaret replying to this letter of Walt's, she had a written exchange with Pat that all but confirmed her doubts. So, on September 7$^{th}$, she wrote to Walt in urgency, asking him to send a few samples so she could ascertain their nature, determine if they had potential, and plan the agenda for the next year accordingly. Walt, by that time, had already gotten his samples to New York via an agent of Lloyd's Film Storage since he himself did not have the money to go and meet distributors in case such a necessity came up. He promptly instructed the agent to take it to Winkler.

Meanwhile, Walt was getting impatient due to having no interesting work. So, he decided not only to pitch more ideas to more people but also prepare in case someone bought his idea, and he went about setting up a rudimentary studio in Robert's garage. He bought a second-hand Pathé camera that was literally falling apart, it was so old. He also went to Alexander Pantages, the Greek owner of Pantages Theatre, with the idea of making short weekly joke reels on the most discussed events of the time, quite similar to the Newman's Laugh-O-Grams, to be shown at his theater with the Pantages brand name advertised heavily across it. Pantages liked the idea and asked Walt to make a sample. He started working on them in the garage studio but soon realized the studio was not conducive to his work.

So, he went out and found himself a room at the back of the real estate office of McRae & Abernathy at a discounted rate of five dollars per month. Of course, Walt once again did not have the money to pay for it and had to borrow $75 from Carl Stalling to provide for it. On October 15$^{th}$, 1923, exactly a week after that, he received a telegram from Margaret that made him think it was all too good to be true. She said that she was ready to work with him on *Alice*. She expected him to improve the quality of his shooting of the child actor and asked for his "cooperation" to market *Alice* since it was a new series with a new name and would require extensive, aggressive, and capital-intensive marketing for it to be received well by the public. But perhaps the one thing that totally made Walt look twice was the remuneration he was being offered for his work. Margaret wanted Walt to make twelve cartoon episodes of *Alice* in total, and she agreed to pay him $1,500 for each of the first six and $1,800 for each of the next six. She wanted Disney to deliver the first one by December 15th, with negatives as well as a poster sketch. Margaret also promised that she would be making the payment for the first six immediately upon receiving the negatives.

Needless to say, this was a bolt out of the blue for Walt, albeit a pleasant one. He sent a telegram back immediately, accepting the offer and asking until January 1st for the first reel. He was so excited that he took a bus to the Sawtelle hospital Roy was in as soon as he had sent the reply to Margaret, even though he reached it nearly at midnight. He had to sneak in and seek his way to Roy's bed. Walt woke his brother up and showed him the offer letter, asking for his help. Roy, too, was excited by the lucrative offer and agreed immediately. Against medical advice, Roy decided to discharge himself from the hospital to get the business started. They would name it the Disney Brothers Cartoon Studio, with Walt being the creative personnel and Roy being the manager of the studio. All their earnings were to be split in half. In a way, it was good that Walt brought Roy on—Walt's lack of business skills and instinct was what led to his previous ventures failing, but Roy's managerial and financial skills would do him good this time.

Walt soon received a sales contract from Winkler, not only extending the deadline to what Walt had asked for but also keeping the road open for a further 24 shorts, twelve each for 1925 and 1926. But financing the project was still a problem for the Disneys. No bank agreed to give them a loan because they were a fledgling venture with no certainty of success. In their emergency, they turned to Robert, who was reluctant at first. For one, at least according to

Walt, Robert was kind of an egotistical person who did not feel very kindly toward him. Secondly, he knew about Walt's tendency to not repay loans, especially with family members. Lastly, like the banks, he was unsure how solid their project was or what their chances of success were. But he might have been convinced when he saw the contract as proof that the brothers were going to be paid well. The brothers then hired their first employee, 16-old Kathleen Dollard, on October 16th to ink and paint cels for them. He also wrote to Margaret Davis, Virginia's aunt, who had played her mother in the original film, asking her to bring Virginia to Hollywood so she could continue starring in the *Alice* cartoons. He offered her a handsome salary of $100 for the first short, which he would slowly increase to $200 by the end of the sixth film and then pay her $250 for the next six. For this, Virginia would have to sign a contract to work with him for a year on the twelve shorts, although she was free to do any other work in between as long as it did not clash with his own project.

Mrs. Davis, though, did not need much convincing like the rest. She had already been trying to get Virginia into Hollywood but hadn't had much success, and she felt like this was the best opportunity for her. On top of that, Virginia had suffered from two bouts of pneumonia in the recent past and had been advised to live in a place with a drier climate, and California would be perfect for that. By October 24th, Walt had signed and sent over his contract with Winkler, and by October 28th, Margaret Davis had accepted the offer for Virginia. By early November, work was already underway on the first of the six cartoons, *Alice's Day at Sea*. Walt used Robert's house as Alice's home in the film, and even Robert's dog Peggy was cast in the film. Two fishermen at the beach in Santa Monica, where they shot the live-action parts, were cast as the sailors. Boxes and cartons had to be used to form animating desks and camera stands, and the camera itself, which was hardly new, had to be operated by Roy since Walt was directing. In fact, Walt had to tutor him in its operation. Having no one to help, Walt had to do the thousands of drawings for the cartoon himself. They were a far cry from the advanced equipment and experienced staff that Walt had wanted, but at least he had work that would bring certain pay and would not fail midway.

The best thing about having his older brother as the manager and bookkeeper was that not only was Roy meticulous in recording each and every expense, no matter how small, but he also had a say in how Walt spent all the money. By this time, the rent at the McRae & Abernathy space had tripled to fifteen dollars, and the brothers had also moved to an apartment that was closer to the studio. However, they did not stay there for long, and come December, they had moved to a cheaper single-room flat in a boarding house opposite their uncle's house that only cost them fifteen dollars a month. They also started eating at a cheap cafeteria nearby instead of having Roy cook as he had before. Another important development around this time was the fact that Margaret Winkler had gotten married to her fiancé Charles Mintz on November 24th, 1923. While this did not affect the Disneys in any way at that moment, it would go on to create severe problems later and prove to be a blessing in disguise for Walt.

The expenses of the Disney Brothers Cartoon Studio increased slowly, as did the loans they were taking. In December, they borrowed $75 twice from Robert, which brought the total of the unpaid debt to him to $500. They also took $50 from another uncle of theirs, $200 each from Carl Stalling and Margaret Davis, $25 from Edna, and $2,500 from the mortgage Elias and Flora Disney took on their Portland house. The brothers had also gotten a new employee, Ann Loomis, on December 8th to assist Kathleen Dollard in her work, and rented a lot at 4589 Hollywood Boulevard for ten dollars a month. Funnily enough, *Alice's Day at Sea* was wrapped up and sent to Winkler on December 15th, the date that she had initially stipulated but one that Walt did not think he could make. Winkler received it on December 26th and promptly proceeded to send them their payment, as well as feedback on the short itself. The Disneys had made a 100% profit on the film—they had spent $750 and earned a profit of $750. Winkler asked Walt to improve on the subject and content of the film, mainly the humor that was used, which was an important factor when it came to short subjects like these. They had also started working on the next cartoon, *Alice Hunting in Africa*. Their production costs were higher for this one, perhaps in a bid to ensure the quality that Walt had promised Winkler. So, even though Winkler sent an advance for the production of the cartoon on January 12th, 1924, when the boys tried to repay Robert his loan of $500 along with the pre-decided eight percent interest of $28.66, they had to come back to him that very day for another loan of $100.

On January 14th, 1924, there was a new entrant to the studio. Walt and Roy, while looking for a third inker and painter to ease their load, hired 24-year-old Lillian Marie Bounds, the youngest sister of Kathleen's friend Hazel Bounds Sewell. While this sounds like a commonplace incident, the fact that Lillian would one day go on to be Mrs. Walt Disney is what made this recruitment a special one. Lillian was out of college and living with her sister, and she took the fifteen-dollar-a-week job because it was only two miles from where she lived, and she would not have to take a bus to get there. One could almost call it love at first sight. Walt started wooing her and was soon giving her rides home after late nights in his and Roy's shared Ford, doing the same for Kathleen so as not to raise unnecessary questions. Lillian was bowled over by his "enthusiasm and optimism," while Walt loved that she would listen patiently to all his rambles about his work and the future of the studio. But Walt was somewhat reluctant to meet with Lillian's family because he did not have a suit, and the car was not really nice either. So, one day, Walt and Roy went down to get proper suits. Walt bought a $40 double-breasted somber green suit to go meet the Sewell family. There might have been awkwardness initially, but once he settled in, there was no going back.

Another event had been happening parallelly with Walt's success in Kansas City that would take a long time to get solved. It all started on October 4th, 1923, when the Laugh-O-Gram Studio went into bankruptcy due to Ub Iwerks filing for a creditor's petition. Ub expressed in his application the desire to use the money due to be received from Pictorial to be used to pay off all the creditors, but he feared that John Schmeltz might stand in the way due to the chattel mortgage that bound the contract to him. After month-long negotiations with Pictorial NY, to which Pictorial Clubs, Inc., the Tennessee branch with which Walt had made the contract, was annexed due to insolvency, Pictorial ended up having to pay the outstanding amount to the studio and, in turn, would earn the right to the six films they had commissioned, *Alice's Wonderland* and the "Lafflets." But as Ub had rightly deduced, Schmeltz would not take things lying down and went on to file an intervening petition on August 15th, 1924. A judge eventually ruled that Schmeltz's claims on the contract were not valid and subsequently recovered and liquidated the assets of Laugh-O-Gram Studio to pay off all the creditors. The case was fully resolved on August 23rd, 1927.

Walt had been asked on January 10th, 1924, by Margaret to quote the lowest possible price for *Alice's Wonderland* to keep as a sort of backup, in case some emergency resulted in Walt not being able to deliver a cartoon. But after enquiring, Walt found out that the film had gone to Pictorial in the bankruptcy dealings and relayed that to Margaret. He also complained about Margaret's very low offer of $300. He told her to contact William Kelley of Pictorial, with whom the original deal had been made, for the reel but also warned her that the price might be too low for Pictorial to accept. Margaret argued that the price was acceptable, given that she may never actually use it. Walt inquired nonetheless and found out that Pictorial had, in all probability, destroyed the negatives. In a way, Walt was relieved. The film, of course, was restored and later added as a bonus feature in the Special Un-Anniversary Edition of Alice in Wonderland on DVD on March 30th, 2010. Also, when it was aired on *Vault Disney*, which aired on Disney Channel in the late 1990s to early 2000s, a thirty-second conjectural ending was added to the film to make up for the ending that was lost in the last-known surviving print, taking the length of the 12-minute print that could be salvaged to 12 minutes and 30 seconds.

*Alice Hunting in Africa* was finished on January 21st, and they had already started making the fourth installment of the series, *Alice's Spooky Adventure*. Margaret, while appreciating Walt's improvements, did ask for better humor and story. *Alice's Spooky Adventure* did have a larger cast, comprised mainly of children from around the neighborhood, who were paid fifty cents per day to be extras in the film. While Walt was working on the animation in February, he decided to hire an animator to share the workload. Thus, 25-year-old Rollin Clare "Ham" Hamilton was hired on February 11th. He worked on *Alice's Spooky Adventure* with Walt, finishing it by February 22nd and starting work on the next one, *Alice's Wild West Show*. Two days later, they shifted to a proper studio space just next door for $35 monthly and set up the office at a garage for $7 monthly. On March 1st, 1924, the first of the *Alice Comedies*, *Alice's Day at Sea*, was finally released in a theater by Winkler Productions to satisfactory reception. Winkler decided to release a short on the first of every month to create good buzz.

Around this time, Margaret, still unsure as to how long she would be able to hold onto the Felix the Cat series, instructed Disney to include a black cat, in the likes of Felix, in his cartoons and let him engage in any kind of surreal shenanigans as he may like. She also started the *Krazy Kat* series at this time. It showed how desperate she was to have a good backup in case Pat pulled the plug on Felix. Thus, the cat that Disney had used in the Laugh-O-Grams for Pictorial started making a regular appearance in the *Alice Comedies*, starting with *Alice's Spooky Adventures* and then again in the fifth film, *Alice's Fishy Story*. Winkler did manage to get Pat to renew his contract on May 1st, but he left for good in 1925, so Winkler's apprehensions did turn out to be right.

Work was delayed on the sixth cartoon, *Alice and the Dog Catcher*, due to an epidemic of foot and mouth disease that broke out in California, which called for an animal quarantine and prevented the studio from using the large number of dogs that was needed for the picture. It was only in May, when the quarantine was lifted, that Walt could resume work, asking for a couple of extra weeks to finish it. *Alice and the Dog Catcher* was an important milestone for the Disney studio, as its cast included Walt and Ham in the main negative roles. It was also the last film Walt animated himself.

In the meantime, Walt, having the money to be able to pay for his staff, started thinking about bringing his Laugh-O-Gram colleagues in. Ub Iwerks, Hugh Harman, Rudy Ising, and "Max" Maxwell were still in Kansas City at this time. Ub and Hugh were working at the Kansas City Film Ad Company. Rudy was working in a Kodak finishing business, and Max was finally going to college. Hugh, Rudy, and Max were working on their own animated series, *Arabian Nights Cartoons: A Thousand and One Laughs* by now and were trying to get Winkler to support their first film, *Sinbad the Sailor*. In May 1924, Ub also expressed the wish to leave his job at the Film Ad Company and join Walt in his new studio. In the meantime, the team at LA was making the next film, *Alice the Peacemaker*, with a new member, 22-year-old Romanian Mike Marcus, who was the cameraman. Walt felt it was only fair that now that they were established enough, they should use a professional animation cameraman instead of trying to cut costs.

## Chapter 7: Famous in LA

By the summer of 1924, Walt Disney was making quite a name for himself around LA. Walt was getting good reviews everywhere, not only because of the novel way he combined animation and live-action but also because of the fact that he was the only major player in LA at this time. Ub had, by this time, reached LA with his mother. He made it there around the middle of July, in spite of Walt requesting him to come earlier at the beginning of June. Ub joined the studio officially as an animator on July 23$^{rd}$, becoming the second animator after Ham. Ub was, undoubtedly, a much better animator than Walt, and with his arrival, Walt officially bid farewell to his own animation career. In a way, he was much more successful and satisfied in writing the content, directing the films, and producing the cartoons. Ub started at $40 a week, lower than his Kansas Film Ad Company's $50 salary but higher than anybody else at the studio. In fact, Walt also raised Ham's salary to $20 to bring them somewhat on par. Ub, ever the innovator, installed a motor drive to the animation camera, doing away with the hand-cranking mechanism, which made the shooting much smoother.

*Alice the Peacemaker* was done around this time, and after Ub arrived, *Alice Gets in Dutch* started production. This film marked the end of using live-action judiciously in the *Alice Comedies*. Walt opined that the live-character-in-animated-world trope had been used long enough and that it was time to move on to more animation-intensive cartoons. It was the right time to do so, too, now that Ub was there to assist him. Ub not only did the animation, but he also resumed his lettering work, doing the posters, titles, and inter-scene title cards. Moreover, it also marked the recurring appearance of the cat modeled on Felix. Until then, it had either been unnamed, variously named, or missing, like in *Alice and the Dog Catcher*. It got its own name, Julius, and an independent personality.

As the year rolled on, Charles Mintz became more and more prominent within Winkler Productions, and soon, he was the one corresponding with the Disneys. Walt credited Mintz's perfectionism with being the reason for Walt developing an almost obsessive drive for quality, which would go on to earn him the reputation of a taskmaster later in life. In fact, *Alice Hunting in Africa*, which Margaret had informed them earlier that she would not release due to being sub-par unless the Disneys edited and polished it, was taken up with renewed interest by Mintz. He pressed them to get it remade and even sent in George Winker, Margaret's brother, to oversee it. Unfortunately, Mintz's constant drive for quality pushed the Disneys to overspend, eliminating profit and ultimately causing a loss of $45.54 with *Alice the Peacemaker*. Walt was once again moving toward the kind of precarious situation he had faced in Kansas City, not only asking Mintz to send over their advance prior to the stipulated time but also holding off on the salaries of employees and asking for financial help from people.

As a last measure, Walt decided, with Mintz's blessing, to not include a live-action opening and closing sequence in *Alice and the Three Bears*, as they incurred an extra cost. Charles liked the end result because it allowed more comic gags to be included. However, he kept pushing Walt to remake *Alice Hunting in Africa*, asking Walt to use live child actors in the films again, thus preserving the live-action part, as well as asking him to fix other fundamental flaws with the combination of the live actor, i.e., Alice, with the animated world.

The Disneys soon hired another animator, 21-year-old Thurston Harper, Jr., in October as they started working on *Alice the Piper*. This started a sort of tug-of-war of personalities within the studio. While Thurston seemed to fit in well with everyone else in the studio, he and Walt just seemed unable to get along with each other. Thurston's raging temper when he lost it did not seem to help either. It was also during this time that Walt finally redid *Alice Hunting in Africa*, but he had an ulterior motive to it. Besides reworking some of the animated parts, he also replaced some of the live-action bits. He made *Alice the Piper* without live-action, meaning that although Alice was a live-action actor, the background was placed in the cartoon world. Using both as his arguments, he tried to convince Charles once again to let him drop the live-action so he would be able to concentrate his focus and resources on the animated parts. This time, George endorsed him, but he also warned him to up the ante on the comedy and content. On the personal front, though, Walt was having a rosy time. He had bought a dark grey second-hand Ford Moon Roadster so that he could take Lillian out himself instead of asking the Davises every time for their Cadillac.

As the eleventh movie in the *Alice Comedies*, *Alice Cans the Cannibals,* was about to air, and as the end of the current contract was drawing near, Walt became impatient regarding the future of the series. He sent a letter to Charles Mintz, asking if they were willing to continue as Margaret had initially promised. Charles wrote back in the affirmative on December 8th and sent George Winkler on December 14th to finalize a deal. The contract Charles put forth promised the studio $1,800 for each short from the thirteenth episode, as had been promised by Margaret, and the brothers accepted it on December 31st. The increased earnings encouraged the Disney duo to finally start giving themselves a salary, at $50 a week each, so that they would no longer have to rely on their uncle Robert.

As the New Year rolled in, it brought a major change in the *Alice Comedies*, too. *Alice Gets Stung*, the third film of 1925, was the last one featuring Virginia Davis (although they would release a previously shot film that had her in it). This was due to the fact that Charles decided they were paying Virginia too much for too little and pressured the Disneys into drawing up a new contract for her, where she would be exclusively "at their beck and call" for the contract period but only be paid for the few days she worked. The Davises, however, did not blame Walt at all, even though things got strained; in fact, they were sympathetic since they saw how Mintz kept cutting into their budget while demanding better and more. When Mrs. Davis protested against those terms to Charles, he simply told her Virginia was important but not indispensable to the series. The Davises even suspected that Charles had another actor ready to take Virginia's place if she left.

The one who did end up taking her place was Marjorie Gossett, aka Margie Gay. She came on with *Alice Solves the Puzzle* and was replaced in the very next one, *Alice's Egg Plant*, by Dawn Paris, aka Dawn O'Day. With an increasing workload due to Winkler Productions trying to enforce the bi-monthly release schedule, the Disneys decided to raise Ub's salary to $50 and Ham's to $30. *Alice's Egg Plant* also marked the naming of Julius, the cat, onscreen. Dawn did not last more than one film most likely because, quite rightly, her mother did not accept the terms of the contract, which was the same as the Davises had been offered. So, they went back to Margie Gay for *Alice Loses Out*; she was the actor who would thus end up doing the most of the *Alice Comedies*, thirty. The next film, *Alice Gets Stage Struck*, was the last one to feature live-action sequences at the beginning and end.

But on the personal front, things were going better. Roy decided to finally propose to Edna, who he had been engaged to for five years, and soon after, when out car-shopping, Walt proposed to Lillian as well. This was something that became a matter of great humor in the family because Walt got teased that he married Lillian because he hated to live alone, because he needed a cook, and because he owed Lillian a lot of money. In a way, that was true because the brothers would often ask her not to cash her check as soon as she got it because they were very often short. The brothers themselves often did not pick up all of their salaries either because they felt the studio needed it more. This continued in 1926 when Charlie Mintz was at his worst with his budget-cutting tendencies. Edna and Roy got married on April 11th, 1925, at the brothers' uncle Robert's house. Walt and Lillian, on the other hand, got married on July 13th in Lewiston, Idaho, at her brother's house. They honeymooned in Mt. Rainer National Park, returning to LA only after August started. They went up to Portland to meet Walt's parents, and when they came back, they moved into a one-room apartment. Lillian had also left working for the studio, except in cases of emergencies, on June 1st. She said later on that she was bad as both an inker and a secretary, so it was probably for the best. But Walt did not change, even as a newly married man. He kept staying at the studio late, often forgetting he had a wife back home now. Sometimes he would return home from the studio or be out with his wife or friends and just leave to go back to the studio to finish a job.

The studio itself was going through some major upheavals. After Kathleen Dollard had left earlier in the year, the Disneys hired Hazelle Linston on May 23rd in the same capacity, who stayed for seven months. Lillian left, and the Disneys' sister, Ruth, joined the studio for seven months on June 23rd, and Ham's sister also joined on June 30th for six months. But for Walt, the best had been the coming of Hugh and Walker Harman and Rudy Ising to the studio as animator, cameraman, and inker, respectively. Walt had been advocating for them to come for far too long, and he was elated. Mike Marcus, a cameraman, had also left the studio, and Rudy not only took his place but would also print, edit, and occasionally animate. Hugh was paid $45 a week, and Rudy got $35. Soon, in early July, Walt increased his own salary to $75. With a much greater population at the studio now, the Disneys decided that it was time to shift to a larger space. They pinpointed a place in 2719 Hyperion Avenue; this space came to be known as the Hyperion Studio.

*Alice Chops the Suey*, which was being made while Walt was still away on his honeymoon, used the lightning sketch technique, something that was renewed as Walt's old staff re-entered the scene. *Alice in the Jungle*, which had already been in the works in September, used footage of Virginia from *Alice Hunting in Africa* instead of Margie, and was, thus, the last *Alice* film she officially appeared in. Winkler Productions, meanwhile, had lost their chance to get back Felix the Cat when the New York Supreme Court ruled in favor of Pat Sullivan going with Educational Pictures for the rest of Felix. On top of that, they were not happy that the studio had failed to deliver on time due to their personal reasons, so Walt had to propose bonuses to get his team to finish the next film ahead of time. As further motivation, he raised the salaries of his main men.

This, however, backfired because Charles Mintz felt that Walt was sending him the films too soon for it to be feasible for Charles to pay. And thus started a long spat between the two regarding the price Charles would pay for the films. Charles tried to lower the price to $1,500, down from $1,800, in exchange for a share of the profits above a certain value, which kept changing as the negotiations advanced. Walt tried to wrestle for a higher price or a higher share of the profits, but Charles kept denying him with the excuse of signing with a national distribution company that would not pay him until the deal start date. This continued until February 1926 when they came to a middle ground. The Disney Brothers Cartoon Studio would be delivering 26 more films in total, starting from March. The first thirteen would be delivered over three weeks, with $900 being paid on receipt and $600 within the next sixty days, and the next thirteen were to be delivered every two weeks, with payment of $900 on receipt and $600 within ninety days. Once the profits reached $4,000, Walt would be getting the first $500 and Charles the next, after which profits would be shared equally. As the altercation came to an end, the studio was also nearly done shifting to their Hyperion location. They had rented a Ford truck for moving, but the day chosen to do so was poor timing since there was a huge rainstorm that day, making everything wet and unusable until it dried.

# Chapter 8: Foray into the Big Leagues

Although the team had moved to the Hyperion Studio at the end of February 1926, the building would not be entirely ready until another two months, as the painting, decorating, and landscaping had yet to be done. Walt also had a little structure made for himself in the vacant area behind the building to store all the old films, as well as the outdoor set for *Alice*. When they came there, it was unanimously agreed upon, in spite of some disagreement, that the name of the studio would be changed from Disney Brothers Cartoon Studio to Walt Disney Studio. Accounts differ regarding whether Roy took this well or whether there was some bitterness regarding the name, but the fact that the change was made and that Roy continued working for the studio suggests that any problems the brothers might have had were more or less solved.

*Alice's Little Parade* had been finished in December 1925, after which Thurston Harper, Jr., left, and *Alice's Mysterious Mystery* in January. While *Alice's Monkey Business* and *Alice in the Wooly*

*West* was being made in February, the ill relations between Walt and Charles Mintz reared its head again when Charles, in no kind terms, criticized *Alice's Mysterious Mystery* for being nothing out of the ordinary and once again pushed for the inclusion of more live-action in the films. Charlie also sent in the contract via George, whose terms did not suit Walt. On top of that, Winkler Productions, having found out that Pictorial had also been distributing cartoons with Alice and many of the cartoons from the *Alice Comedies* appeared in it, albeit marketed with different names and looks, they started suspecting that perhaps Walt had made himself seem more than what he really had been—not the owner of Laugh-O-Gram but only a creator under it. They tried to get the upper hand over Walt by accusing that he had no claim over the name *Alice Comedies*. But Walt kept trying to get them to accept his terms, so Charles went to LA on March 24th, 1926, to clear the confusion, and they not only signed a contract but also a written agreement that clearly stated that Winkler Productions would continue to retain their interest in *Alice* and have 50% ownership over the *Alice Comedies* name if the option for more seasons of *Alice* was exercised as per the contract, even after they were done with the 26 promised. In fact, things improved so far as to allow Charles to praise their latest, *Alice the Fire Fighter*, as the best short they had turned in yet when he got it in May.

About August, Hugh Harman and Rudy Ising, along with "Max" Maxwell, who was still in Kansas City, started making plans to leave the Walt Disney Studio and form their own studio. In fact, this had always been their plan, even as they were coming to LA on Walt's insistence. They had only meant to stay a year with Walt to learn the ropes of the trade in LA until they could be their own masters. Hugh and Rudy were even in talks by August with Jesse Lasky, a producer, regarding this. Walt, too, had been looking elsewhere. He started production on a second film for Dr. Thomas McCrum, with whom he had been in contact during his time in LA. It was called *Clara Cleans Her Teeth* and featured an actual professional cast. The

Disney brothers were also well-off enough by now to build their own houses. Construction took from August to December and cost them $16,000, an amount that cut their net worth back by a chunk.

As per their contract, *Alice Charms the Fish* was released in September. It was the first *Alice* film that was released to nationwide audiences since Winkler Productions had only been a states' rights distributor. Something else was also happening around this time. Walt, as a reward or maybe a break, gave a holiday of two weeks to all his studio members. However, Hugh and Rudy saw this as an opportunity to further their own interests. Bringing Ub and Ham on board due to their animation skills, they decided to use the equipment at the studio while it was empty to make the sequel to *Sinbad*, called *Aladdin's Vamp*. But for this reason or that, they failed to find anyone to release it. However, in all probability, Walt got a whiff of their divergence because, out of the blue, he decided to raise the salaries of both Ub and Hugh to the uncharacteristically high values of $75 and $60. He also hired a new painter, twenty-year-old Paul Smith, who even started animating after some time. While that kept them within the fold, it put Walt and Roy in tight corners as the net profits on each film kept getting slimmer, from around $600 in 1925 to hardly $100 toward the end of 1926, even though they were making as much as $1,800 to $2,000 per film due to the profit-sharing arrangement.

A lot of unexpected changes came about on the last day of 1926. A conflict with Walt made Ham leave the studio as they started work on *Alice's Circus Daze*, which starred yet another new actor as Alice. On the insistence of George Winkler, twelve-year-old Lois Hardwick came on board, even though they were doing quite well with Margie. This created some friction among people, mainly due to a lack of communication between Charles and George. Charles had presumed Walt had gone over him to make the hire, but Walt quickly straightened out the situation, causing Charles to adopt a more placating tone, even giving more independence to Walt and George to make their own decisions. Perhaps this was due to the fact that Walt's cartoons were actually quite good and more profitable than they had been before. However, one person who remained skeptical was Virginia Davis. After she was grown enough to understand, she would keep saying how generic and insignificant Alice's role had become. When Lois came on, she criticized how she was too old for the role.

Disney's star animator Ub Iwerks got married to Mildred Henderson on January 5$^{th}$, 1927. Ten days later, while Ub was on his honeymoon, Walt hired a new animator for the two he lost, Isadore "Friz" Freleng, who was also from the Kansas City Film Ad Company. Freleng would go on to help develop some of the major stars of *Loony Tunes*, including Bugs Bunny, Porky Pig, Tweety, and Yosemite Sam. Walt also took on an assistant animator by the name of Norman Blackburn and hired twenty-year-old Leslie "Les" Clark. The hiring spree of February ended with Ben Clopton, who also became an assistant animator. Around the same time, the young Disney couples moved into their respective houses, and soon afterward, Lillian's mother moved in with Walt and Lillian.

Ever since the year had begun, Rudy had been quite driven in trying to set up his own shop. He had talked about a secret studio somewhere that was all equipped and ready to be used as soon as a contract could be won. He and Hugh even wrote to Max, assuring him that they would not take long since they had been in talks with MGM, Fox, Universal, and Paramount. In a way, Rudy got his wish fulfilled in March itself when he was let go by Walt for falling asleep between frames while shooting the animations.

Another turning point now came for Walt Disney Studio. Toward the end of January 1927, even as Walt was busy with *Alice*, Charles Mintz asked Walt to design a new character, a rabbit, for a new animated series that they might be doing with Universal. Carl Laemmle, the founder of Universal Pictures, had asked for a new animated series with a rabbit because "there were too many darn cats in cartoons." So, everyone who could draw at Walt Disney Studio made sketches of rabbit cartoons according to their own ideas, and

Walt sent these into Charles. When Universal greenlit them, Charles signed a contract with Universal for 26 films featuring this rabbit. The name Oswald was chosen by literally drawing names suggested by employees out of a hat. Perhaps this is why the name does not have the alliterative nature that other cartoon characters often had, like its successor Mickey Mouse itself, Donald Duck, or Bugs Bunny. Around the middle of March, Charles traveled to LA to see Walt in person and negotiate funds, which was concluded at a $2,250 advance for each short to be delivered for a September 1st release. So, even as the last of the *Alice Comedies* were being produced in March, most of the time and energy at the studio was being devoted to Oswald the Lucky Rabbit. Although Charles was far less rude to Walt than he used to be, he was still his pushy self, as he kept asking Walt to finish on time, to keep sending him the animation drawings, and to also send him the names and subjects of the first few films they had planned. To cope with the added pressure, Walt re-hired Mike Marcus as a cameraman, hired Lillian's sister, Hazel, as the inking and painting supervisor, and started raising Ub's pay to the point that it would reach a whopping $120 in a couple of months.

*Poor Papa* was the first of the Oswald films shot by Disney. It was sent over to Charles on April 10th, but both he and Universal heavily criticized it. They felt that Oswald looked too old and round, that there was not much focus on the central character, and that the character had no unique personality. Universal even went so far as to say that the quality of animation, as well as the content, was not good enough. It is well known that Charles had asked Walt to give Oswald a monocle, which Walt flat-out refused. He did give Oswald a makeover, though, and tried to improve the story, but he also did not agree with a lot of the criticisms. So, when the second short, *Trolley Troubles*, was being written, Walt did it through a brainstorming session, where whoever came up with a gag worthy of being added to the final cut would be given $5. This is the film that contains the very popular scene of Oswald taking off his foot to rub on his back, a nod to a common tradition of keeping a rabbit's foot with oneself for luck. *Trolley Troubles* was sent over on May 1st with promises of further improvements to the character and animation technique.

To keep that promise, Walt kept hiring more and more animators. Ham returned at this time, Max came over from Kansas City to join the bunch, and another newbie, 21-year-old Ray Abrams, came on board. Walt also routinely held brainstorming sessions to improve on the story. In the meantime, Universal was marketing Oswald quite aggressively, getting ads up wherever they could and putting his name and face on everything from candy bars to merchandise. They also decided to premiere the series with *Trolley Troubles* since *Poor Papa* did not match up to the standards they envisioned. It was released first at the Criterion Theatre in LA on the Fourth of July and nationally on Labor Day, all to rave reviews, even as Alice got a quiet goodbye with *Alice in the Big League* on August 22nd, 1927.

The breakout popularity of Oswald prompted Walt to reorganize the studio. He formed the staff into animation teams, with Ub and Friz on one and Hugh and Ham on another, with Paul, Ben, Norm, Les, and Johnny Cannon, a new member, forming the lower-tier group. Brainstorming sessions became common, and bonuses were given out for great ideas and finishing on schedule. But all was not well. Walt's taskmaster's attitude did not sit well with his staff, and they were discontented to the point that most of them considered leaving, especially after Walker Harman actually left. Friz had always had friction with Walt because he had been bullied as a kid and a teen and did not like how Walt bulldozed over everybody's needs and desires. Hugh and Max already had their own plans with Rudy, while the others simply wanted a healthier environment where they were more appreciated. Ub was perhaps the only one with no intention to defect with Winkler Productions but did plan to build his own independent business.

At this time, around the middle of 1927, gasoline was added to the fire when Charles Mintz decided to go behind Walt's back and take

Oswald for himself. He sent George Winkler to assess the general consensus within the studio about breaking away when he went to drop the check off and pick up the reels. He talked to Hugh, and when Charles learned that a lot of the staff would be interested in such a move, he started calling them up and meeting them discreetly in LA to discuss the matter over. Margaret Winkler and Charles Mintz felt that the Disneys were too bratty and demanding to work with, and as soon as the present contract expired, they would take Oswald into their own hands under George Winkler. Coincidentally, the day *Trolley Troubles* released nationwide, Friz was kicked out of the studio for skipping work to go to the movies. The Oswald shorts continued to be released, all to rave reviews, and Oswald became so popular that he started to rival established characters like Felix the Cat. Money started pouring in, so much so that the brothers could afford to buy ten acres of land and invest in the oil business, and Ub was able to buy stone mills to work on his renowned paint formulae with. The brothers were also able to add more staff to the team and increase their own salaries to $100 for Walt and $65 for Roy. Their profits soared again, with $500 per film, and their year-end profits were $8,935.

At the last leg of the first series of Oswald, which was at the beginning of 1928, Charles Mintz signed a three-year contract with Universal for Oswald. Walt was so blinded by the possibility of working on Oswald until 1931 that even when Ub warned Walt what Charles and George were plotting with his very own staff behind his back, he refused to acknowledge it. Even Rudy, who had been trying hard to get a contract with another studio since late 1927, was all geared to sign a contract with Winkler Productions, along with Hugh, Ham, and Max. But Walt, in his giddiness at his success, decided to go meet Charles in New York anyway to see if he could get a raise to $2,500 per short so that he could churn out even better films. Walt was wary, though, and took with him some of the Oswald shorts and review clippings to try and see if he could get another distributor to work with him. He left for New York with

Lillian on February 21st and got in touch with John Alicoate, the publisher and manager of *Film Daily*. Alicoate advised Walt that if he planned to get another distributor, then he should try MGM or Fox but should not give up on Charles yet. Walt did try to convince both studios, but ultimately, they refused, with MGM saying Oswald was too short a film to earn them the profits they envisioned and Fox saying that they did not distribute films they did not produce themselves. In the meantime, Walt was also talking with Bill Nolan, the creator of the *Krazy Kat* cartoons, and convinced him to come work for Walt Disney Studio. Walt also told Roy to draw up contracts for his staff to sign so that it would be clear who was planning to leave. By this time, Roy had already sacked Max, and when the contracts were presented, Hugh, Ham, Paul, Norm, Ben, and Ray openly defected, while Ub, Les, and Johnny stayed loyal.

In the meantime, Walt also started visiting Universal as a last-ditch effort to see if he could deal directly with them. But even though Universal seemed favorable to Walt, they said they could not do anything before a year, as the contract for 1928/29 had already been signed with Charles. They asked him to sort it out with Winkler Productions for a year, after which they might take Disney on directly. Thoroughly disappointed, Walt went back to trying to renegotiate with Charles. But Charles was no longer even trying to hide his motives. He kept lowering his price for Walt, ultimately telling him to take his offer or else Charles would have to take over the production of Oswald. He told Walt that most of his men were ready to come with him, so it would not be a problem. Walt, outraged, called it quits with Charles and left New York on March 13th, after three weeks of a cat-and-mouse game, vowing to never work under anyone ever again. He got sweet revenge when Universal decided to terminate Mintz's contract after 26 more shorts of Oswald to produce it in in-house under Walter Lantz, who would later go on to create Woody the Woodpecker. In a way, that worked out well because it resulted in the birth of Mickey Mouse, Disney's most iconic creation ever.

# Chapter 9: The Birth of Mickey Mouse

Even as Disney was returning home on a train with Lillian, he was wracking his brains for a new cartoon that he could make. He kept coming back to a mouse. The exact reason is unknown, but a popular story goes that he had adopted one of the mice that had used to run wild in the Laugh-O-Gram Studio. He used to keep it in his drawer, calling it Mortimer. It is known that when Walt first created Mickey Mouse, he had wanted to name it Mortimer, but Lillian had convinced him that it was too serious a name and that he should use Mickey instead.

After Disney returned, the team, amidst tangible coldness, completed the five remaining Oswald shorts for the sake of their contract with Mintz, after which, the only ones left in the studio were Ub, Les, Johnny, Lillian, Edna, Hazel, and a new animator named Wilfred Jackson, who joined on April 16th, 1928. Even as Oswald was being produced, Walt separated Ub entirely from the rest, making him work in absolute secrecy to create Mickey, with a little help from Ben. But the renegades did find out later on, courtesy of Ben. The first silent Mickey Mouse cartoon, *Plane Crazy*, which also featured

Minnie Mouse, was released as a test screening on May 15th, 1928, in a theater on Sunset Boulevard; it was heavily based on Charles Lindbergh's transatlantic flight the year before and had cost $1,772.89 to make. The very next day, Walt applied for a trademark on the name Mickey Mouse, knowing fully well what happens if one didn't own the rights to one's characters. The second film, *The Gallopin' Gaucho*, was done in June and July and released in August. But Walt failed to find a distributor for either, and they were flops.

Sound in films was still a novel feature in films at that time, so Disney decided to exploit that. He had finished the silent shooting of *Steamboat Willie* by late August, in which Wilfred had come up with the bouncing ball metronome to help with recording the synchronized sound. Wilfred also worked on the animation with Ub and Les. Walt once again set off for New York, this time to record the sound. On his way, Walt had called on his old friend Carl Stalling in Kansas City to help him with the music on the other two cartoons. Upon reaching New York, Walt looked around and decided to use the Powers Cinephone recording system from Patrick "Pat" Powers of Celebrity Productions. It required several takes before a near-perfect synchronization could be obtained, mainly due to the translation of the Disneys' rudimentary sound sheet to actual musical language and the initial reluctance of the conductor to use the metronome. Walt himself voiced the characters, although there is not much intelligible dialogue, and the background music was "Turkey in the Straw."

With that, Disney set out to look for distributors, but as is with all newcomers, hardly anybody entertained him. On October 26th, 1928, Carl Stalling came to New York to create the music for *Plane Crazy*, *The Gallopin' Gaucho*, and *The Barn Dance*, which was the fourth cartoon that had been made, albeit without Disney. It was around this time that Walt and Roy had to mortgage off their property—Walt even had to sell his car—for the recordings and Carl's hotel expenses.

In November, Harry Reichenbach, the manager of the Colony Theater on Broadway, asked Walt to show *Steamboat Willie* for two weeks at $500. The final amount that Walt got is a mystery, as Walt once said that he had bargained and got $1,000 but later gave a differing statement. However, it did not take Walt much convincing, although he was initially doubtful as to whether this much-needed exposure would lower his chances of getting a distributor. *Steamboat Willie* was novel enough to garner a great reception from the very first day it started showing, which was November 18$^{th}$, 1928, and it ran for thirteen days in total. It might not have been the first cartoon with sound, as Fleischer Studios had already made some in the mid-1920s, and Winkler Productions had also tried to accomplish sound cartoons, albeit to utter failure, but it was still the first that used synced sound.

It allowed Disney to be able to get a distributor. He had already had an agreement with Pat Powers of Celebrity Productions to let him be Walt's agent and find him a distributor. But, as soon as he and Carl left for LA, Powers signed him up with a states' rights distributor, Stanley Warner, with the excuse that getting a national distributor for a new and unknown series was difficult, if not impossible. This put Disney in a precarious position. Not only did it reduce the chances of his exposure, but it would also reduce his chances of a successful national distribution later on if he did manage to sign with any company.

After returning, Carl started working on the sound for the fifth cartoon, *The Opry House*, in December, but it would be an understatement to say that there were disagreements in the studio. Walt and Carl quarreled every day, mostly over Walt's preposterous demands that Carl edit and modify the sound to the animation, even if it was not technically possible. Walt conceded that if Carl managed to listen to Walt on this one, Walt would let Carl have full liberty with the music on every cartoon afterward. It is unknown if Carl succeeded, but the fact that, even before *The Opry House* was finished, production started on *Silly Symphonies*, an idea that had been suggested by Carl way back when Disney came to see him before going to New York, indicates the affirmative. Thus, the first of the *Silly Symphonies*, *The Skeleton Dance*, was made by Ub.

The sound version of *The Gallopin' Gaucho* was first played in New York, on December 30$^{th}$, 1928. Walt and Carl were also back in New York by the end of January to record *The Opry House* and *The Skeleton Dance*. The latter was not even animated yet, but thanks to the metronome system, they could afford to record the sound beforehand, as long as both the animators and music-makers stuck to the meter. To save on costs, Disney was trying to convince Ub, all the way from New York, to use the in-between method, where Ub would only draw the key poses and scenes, leaving the in-between pictures to the assistants. However, Ub wanted to do all of it himself, like before. While Ub's accuracy did help in aligning the music with the animation, it also put too much pressure on him, as he was the lone animator, which made progress slow.

When Walt had returned from New York in March, there had been quite a few changes. For one, Disney opened a short-lived recording studio named Disney Film Recording Company, using equipment purchased from Pat Powers. Walt also started expanding his pinched staff by recruiting animators from New York in April. The first was Ben Sharpsteen, who would go on to direct *Dumbo*, and the other was Burt Gillett, who is most noted for his work on *The Three Little Pigs*. Ub Iwerks thus assumed a greater supervisory role. Initially, roles were interchangeable in the studio, but as more and more animators joined, designations became more concrete. At the lower tiers, employees were separated into painters, inkers, and animators, and on the highest tier, Ub became responsible for the *Silly Symphonies* while Gillett took over *Mickey Mouse*. Walt also signed his men up for an art course at the Chouinard Art Institute in LA for Friday night classes, although how seriously they were taken is a matter of doubt.

On March 17$^{th}$, 1929, the sound version of *Plane Crazy* was released. *The Opry House*, the first film to show Mickey wearing gloves, and *When the Cat's Away* was finished in March and May, respectively. In early May, Disney successfully got the first of the *Silly Symphonies*, *The Skeleton Dance*, shown at the Carthay Circle Theatre in Los Angeles. Encouraged by its regional success, Walt once again pushed to try and get a national distributor for the *Silly Symphonies* based on their great reviews and the acclaim of the popular *Mickey Mouse* films, which finally paid off when they got a Columbia Pictures contract for thirteen *Silly Symphonies* in August.

Meanwhile, the *Mickey Mouse* series was also going in full swing. *The Plowboy* was finished on June 28$^{th}$ and released in July, which featured Horace Horsecollar for the first time and Clarabelle Cow, making this her second appearance. These two characters were actually some of the other ideas that had been suggested until Mickey Mouse had been finalized as the protagonist. On August 12$^{th}$, Walt finally got the trademark for the Mickey Mouse image that he had applied for on June 5$^{th}$.

In September that year, Harry Woodin, a theater manager, gave Walt the ingenious idea of holding Mickey Mouse Club meetings in theaters. These meetings were not like the later television program; in these meetings, they would have viewings of cartoons, play games, and sing songs. This kickstarted Walt's foray into a multi-realm business as he realized the importance of using gimmicks and merchandise to gain popularity. Around this time, Walt decided to do comic strips of Mickey Mouse as well. He assigned Ub to the job of creating samples. In the meantime, more Mickey Mouse movies were being released, like *Mickey's Choo-Choo*, *The Jazz Fool*, and *Jungle Rhythm*. About this time, Disney stumbled upon his first merchandise deal when he struck an agreement with a stationery company for the right to imprint Mickey's image on school writing tablets. On November 18$^{th}$, Walt sent some of the comic strips to King Features for a look-over. The response was positive, as Disney was asked for six more on November 21$^{st}$, which Walt sent on December 18$^{th}$. Soon, King Features asked to let the *New York*

*Mirror* publish *Mickey Mouse* comics starting in January. The first was published on January 13th, and an official deal followed.[2,3]

January of 1930 was actually quite an eventful month. The Mickey Mouse Club debuted at the Fox Dome Theater in Ocean Park, California, on January 11th, and within a couple of months, over sixty theaters were organizing meetings. On the merchandising front, Walt Disney Productions, which had been renamed once again in December 1929, was making great strides as they signed with George Borgfeldt & Company, which produced such items as toys, on February 3rd. April and May were abuzz with Mickey, but Walt's biggest breakthrough came on June 17th when Walt signed a deal to make Mickey merchandise in England, and either at the end of June or the beginning of July, he signed a deal to publish Mickey comics in European newspapers. Mickey also made it to Madame Tussauds in London, where he got his own wax figure.

However, even amidst such massive strides, the mood at the studio was quite melancholic. Soon after, Walt, along with his attorney and Lillian, went to New York to negotiate higher prices with Pat Powers. Once there, he witnessed perhaps his second-biggest betrayal after opening the first Disney studio. This time, the defector was Ub Iwerks himself, who gave his notice to Roy while Walt was away. Not only did Powers cancel any further deals with Walt, but he also made Walt pay $50,000. Ub left to open his own studio, backed by Powers, soon after finishing *The Cactus Kid*, Ub's last Mickey animation. Apparently, Ub had been in talks since September of the previous year and never let on. As soon as Carl Stalling found out about Ub leaving, he made an instant decision to do the same. In the process, they both lost the interests they had in the company, as per their contracts. In a way, it was their loss since

---

[2] http://kpolsson.com/mmouse/

[3] https://www.infoplease.com/spot/mickey-mouse-timeline

both the *Mickey Mouse* films and *Silly Symphonies* kept getting more popular, while the two failed to do anything significant themselves. Walt also signed with Columbia Pictures to distribute Mickey Mouse; he borrowed the money to pay Powers from them, which were to be paid through waived profits on the *Mickey Mouse* films. However, Columbia would still pay Walt Disney Productions $7,000 per film on delivery. The only other silver lining was the publication of *The Mickey Mouse Book*, the first such book of its kind, in October.

It is important to note that around this time, other important characters associated with Mickey Mouse also started making an appearance. The first of these was Pluto. Of the entire Mickey gang, Pluto is the only character that is not anthropomorphic. Just like Julius in the *Alice Comedies*, when the character debuted, he did not have a name. He was only a side character, a bloodhound, in the twenty-first short in the *Mickey Mouse* series *The Chain Gang*, which released in September 1930. His next appearance was in *The Picnic* as Minnie's pet dog Rover that very year. It was only in his next appearance in *The Moose Hunt* the following year that he was given the name Pluto the Pup. The origin of his name, in classic Walt Disney style, was an attempt to cash in on the excitement of the discovery and christening of the ninth planet of our solar system. Goofy also got a similar introduction as an anonymous character in *Mickey's Revue* in May 1932. He was not even called Goofy back then. His name was Dippy Dawg, which was in the same alliterative style as the rest of the main group. But, in July 1932, a Terrytoons animator, Arthur Babitsky, joined the studio. This would not only change the fate of Dippy but also the nature of animation at the studio.

Better known as Art Babbitt, he was highly respected in the animation world for his ability for deep character study. In fact, Babbitt successfully revived the system of art practice and human movement study just a few years after the Chouinard classes had been abandoned by everyone due to apathy with the clever tactic of using nude models. Getting wind, Walt soon shifted the classes from Babbitt's home to the studio premises to avoid a press scandal. Babbitt's talent for intensive character analysis not only elevated Dippy Dawg, an unnamed, unimportant character used only for gags to Goofy, an integral part of Mickey's gang, within just two years with the release of *Orphan's Benefit* in August 1934. *Orphan's Benefit* is also credited with being the first *Mickey Mouse* cartoon to feature Donald Duck. Although it was his second appearance (the first was *The Wise Little Hen* earlier that year, which was a part of the *Silly Symphonies* series), this is the film that gave Donald the look we are more familiar with today. Babbitt had a hand in Donald Duck's development, which is why he has more well-formed character traits. In fact, the main purpose of creating him was to have a more human character since Mickey was supposed to be a role model for children.

Stepping back into the timeline, all through the rest of 1930, as well as 1931, both *Silly Symphonies* and the *Mickey Mouse* films kept gathering star reviews. Walt had also expanded the studio with a quarter-million dollars in the first half of 1931. But somewhere along the line, all the physical and emotional exertion throughout the years had taken a toll on Walt. In October 1931, Walt had a severe nervous breakdown that rendered him unable to function. Gaining a new perspective, he set off on a long soul-searching cross-country vacation to Panama and Cuba with Lillian. It is hard to say how much he actually recovered, but he definitely returned with renewed vigor. The best example of that was with the release of *Flowers and Trees*, a *Silly Symphonies* cartoon and the first full-color film made using three-strip Technicolor released commercially, on July 18$^{th}$, 1932. It won the 1932 Oscar for best "Short Subjects, Cartoons" and was the first animated film to win an Oscar. In fact, every *Silly Symphonies* cartoon received an Oscar from then until 1939, losing out only to *Ferdinand the Bull* in 1938, which was also a Disney product. Walt Disney also received an honorary Academy Award in 1932 for creating Mickey Mouse. To celebrate his success, he built himself a grand new Norman-French style house with twelve rooms and a swimming pool.

# Chapter 10: Disney Movie Magic

Walt experienced great happiness on December 18$^{th}$, 1933, when he welcomed his daughter, Diane Marie, to the world after two failed pregnancies. They did not have any more biological children, as Lillian was advised against it by doctors, but the Disneys would go on to adopt a girl, Sharon Mae, after she was born on December 31$^{st}$, 1936. Within the family, Sharon's adoption was not a hush-hush matter, but Walt consciously did not let it reach the ears of the press, nor did he allow anyone in the family to discuss it with outsiders in a bid to protect their daughter at a time when adoption was still considered to be taboo.[4] Disney was highly protective of his daughters and wanted to give them as normal a family life as possible. It is said that his daughters were the only people in his life he put above his work. Even Lillian knew that if it came to choosing between her and his work, he would choose his work. His employees often said that in spite of all or most of them having no formal training and literally learning everything on the job, Walt revered the work as an art. Many opine that since art had been his only escape or outlet since his lonely, abusive childhood, and he had faced multiple betrayals in his life, he saw his work as the only thing he could bank

---

[4] https://consideringadoption.com/celebrity-adoption/walt-disney-devoted-family-man-and-adoptive-father

on without fear. To him, it was never about earning more money but about reaching greater heights in the field of animation.[5]

In 1932, the "Short Subject (Cartoon)" category was started by the Academy of Motion Picture Arts and Sciences for their fifth award ceremony, a ceremony better known as the Oscars. Disney became the first-ever recipient of the award for his *Flowers and Trees*. When he got it again the next year for *The Three Little Pigs*, he became more serious about the content he was creating. So, he created a separate story department altogether. He had already been using the storyboard for a year now, after serendipitously coming up with it along with Webb Smith, one of his animators. Smith went on to become one of the first members of the story department. The creation of the department and Walt's rapidly growing popularity brought about a change in the dynamics of the studio employees. Walt had already been separating inbetweeners, inkers, and junior animators from the senior animators for some time now, and the story department, which had the highest-ranking artists, made the distinction even more glaring. Earlier, Walt had been known to fraternize well with his employees, playing games with them, visiting their houses, and being on a first-name basis with them. But he was fast becoming a different man, more like a boss and less like one of them. As soon as Walt felt an artist was no longer able to deliver good work, he would let them go, no matter how intimate their association. He was fast losing touch with his own identity, to a point it had, by his own admission, dissociated into two parts—Walt Disney, the brand, and Disney, the man.

And Disney the brand could not be stopped. In 1934, Disney had another idea that would take the animation world by storm. He decided to make a full-length sound and color animated feature film, *Snow White and the Seven Dwarfs*. Though not the first animated full-length film, it definitely was the first one to be done fully using cel animation. It was the decision of a visionary, but at the height of

---

[5] https://www.telegraph.co.uk/culture/3662566/Walt-man-or-mouse.html

the Great Depression, it was labeled by the industry as "Disney's Folly." Disney, of course, did not pay any heed. He went ahead with production, building sets and sending his animators to the Chouinard Art Institute again. He had also, at one point, wanted to get Virginia Davis, who was now grown up, to voice Snow White, but the deal did not come through, and Adriana Caselotti ended up voicing the character. He even had live animals brought to his studio so that the animators could depict the animals in the film realistically. The film cost a whopping $1.49 million to make, quite unimaginable in those days, and took almost four years to complete. Another point in which the film was a pioneer was that it used the multiplane camera on a massive scale. Such a set-up had already been used by Lotte Reiniger for *The Adventures of Prince Achmed*, coincidentally the first feature-length animated film with a surviving print. This set-up was also used by Ub Iwerks and in the Fleischer Studios. In the Disney Studio, it was invented by William Garity.[6] *The Old Mill* was the first film that was shot using it. *Snow White* was nearing completion by this time, but Walt had parts of it redone using the camera. At one point, everyone, from his wife and brother to even his own animators, opposed his fanaticism, fearing it would bankrupt the studio. Disney had to take several loans and even mortgage his house toward the end to be able to finance it. The film ended up earning eight million dollars internationally, and when adjusted for inflation, it is still the highest-grossing animated movie of all time. When it was finally released on December 21st, 1937, the overwhelming response it got helped Disney pay off his debts and get out of the rut he had sunk into. He used the rest of the money to buy a 51-acre plot of land in Burbank, California, while Roy was out of the country, to build a new studio. Walt Disney Films is still situated there today.

Disney wanted to build a much more productive space for his employees. He had air-conditioning installed all throughout the

---

[6] https://en.wikipedia.org/wiki/Multiplane_camera

building. He even had a restaurant, coffee shop, gym, and gas station built within the premises. Needless to say, the expenses shot through the roof. On top of that, he started work on two more animated feature films the next year, *Pinocchio* and *Fantasia*, with *Bambi* still in production. *Fantasia* was Walt's pet project, as he wanted it to be an elongated visual and aural treat along the lines of *The Sorcerer's Apprentice*. Walt was so excited about *Fantasia* that he often neglected *Pinocchio* for it. But the income of the studio was sliding from millions to thousands, so Walt was pushing hard to make them good enough to be as big of a hit as *Snow White*. When *Snow White* received an Honorary Oscar for being the first of its kind and for opening new doors for the animation world, Disney became even more overconfident and hyper-enthusiastic.[7] Although these projects were ambitious, the timing couldn't be more unfortunate. Both the films were released in 1940, as the world was reeling from the breakout of World War II. With the wartime financial crisis plaguing most of the high-revenue countries, the films failed miserably. Unable to sustain themselves any longer, the company started its first public stock offering in 1940 amid mass layoffs and salary cuts. It helped recover some of the losses of the company and paid off almost two million dollars in debts.

Part of this obsession was a result of a tragedy that befell the Disneys in 1938. The brothers had gifted their parents a brand-new house to live in for their fiftieth anniversary. But before the year ended, their mother died. Apparently, there had been some malfunction in the heating system, and Flora died from asphyxiation. Walt, for whom his mother was the only parental figure he felt he received unconditional love from, was devastated. He blamed himself for her death. He was not on good terms with his father anyway, and this further distanced them. It also affected his attitude at the studio. He became high-handed and callous in his dealings with his men. By this time, the staff had moved to the Burbank

---

[7] https://listverse.com/2012/11/05/top-10-ridiculous-disney-movie-flops/

building and were experiencing a worse form of the class segregation that had been present before. The top brass was being allowed to enjoy more of the amenities at the studio than the ones lower down the ranks.[8]

Even the older Disney employees, who had always been somewhat disgruntled by yet mostly forgiving of Walt's ruthless work ethics and detached association with his now huge staff, were getting restless, especially in the face of the salary cuts. Many of his top animators were pushing Walt to allow labor unions, but when Walt flat-out criticized the demand in a February speech to his studio workers, the animators went off to join the Screen Cartoonist's Guild. Walt took offense to this and fired them. The very next day, over 200 of his staff went on a unanimous strike on May 29th, 1941, that lasted about five weeks. During this time, the Office of the Coordinator of Inter-American Affairs advised Walt to make a goodwill tour of South America, which came to be known as the El Grupo tour, until the situation cooled down a little. While he was still on the goodwill tour, his father died. But by this time, Walt was already estranged from his father, and he refused to interrupt the tour to attend his father's funeral.[9] Roy did not object—he felt it would be better if Walt returned after the negotiations were complete, especially in light of the fact that Walt was easily agitated by the situation and had even tried to attack one of his best artists, Art Babbitt, who was the frontman of the protests. After Walt returned, the federal mediator from the National Labor Relations Board was sent to negotiate with Walt and got him to sign a union contract. But he immediately went on to fire most of the animators, including Babbitt, made huge reductions in salary, and restricted the usage of amenities. However, the studio was now understaffed, with little more than half of its previous workforce, which was a great blow to the ongoing production of *Dumbo*. In spite of having a hurried

---

[8] https://www.glamour.com/story/walt-disney-secrets-you-never-knew

[9] https://www.glamour.com/story/walt-disney-secrets-you-never-knew

finish, it received decent reviews upon its release in October. But Walt did not forget or forgive. He held a grudge against the rebelling animators for his great losses for the better part of the decade. After the formation of the Motion Picture Alliance for the Preservation of American Ideals in 1946, with Walt as one of the founding members, he got back at the rebels by claiming the animators' strike was an attempted communist takeover, outright saying that the Screen Cartoonist's Guild was a front for the communists in Hollywood and naming several of the agitators as aides to the House Committee on Un-American Activities in his testimony during the 1947 Red Scare.[10,11]

Walt's vehement opposition for left-wing philosophy and support for right-wing nationalism had been apparent since 1940 when he promptly pulled his support of the Democratic Party in favor of the Republican Party, after Franklin Delano Roosevelt, a supporter of labor unions, was reelected. In December 1941, after the Pearl Harbor attack, Walt opened his studio grounds to around 500 US soldiers who had been on duty at the Lockheed aircraft plant nearby. Disney, ever the businessman, was finding ways to make a profit even amidst the war. He created the Walt Disney Training Films Unit and started making military video manuals and propaganda films, the most notable of which was the Oscar-winning *Der Fuehrer's Face*. But Walt was, after all, an entertainment man. Even though ninety percent of the pictures released by the studio were war films, the rest were purely for entertainment[12] He soon released *Bambi* in 1942, which had been in production since 1937. Unfortunately, it was a misstep, as it tanked at the box office and sunk the studio further into debt. Roy Disney, using his financial prowess, advised Walt to move beyond animated films. Taking heed,

---

[10] Wikipedia for Walt Disney, Disney animators' strike, HUAC and MPAP

[11] https://www.theguardian.com/world/2006/nov/26/film.usa

[12] https://www.waltdisney.org/blog/walt-disney-joins-war-effort-celebrate-us-111111

he started making live-action feature-length films, like *Treasure Island* (1950) and the live-action nature documentary series *True-Life Adventures* (1948-1960). The studio also put out live-action-animated combination films like *Melody Time* (1948) and also made TV productions like *The Mickey Mouse Club* (intermittently through 1955 to 1996).

However, the road was not all rosy. In 1946, he released *Song of the South*, which was heavily criticized for having racist overtones and making use of racial stereotypes; it got to the point that the National Association for the Advancement of Colored People (NAACP) had to get involved several times. Next, in 1950, came *Cinderella*, which was adapted from Charles Perrault's *Cendrillon* and not the Brothers Grimm tale, as many believe. *Cinderella* was a fantasy film involving a princess just like *Snow White* and had the same appeal for post-war Americans, helping to bring in much-needed revenue to save the studio from bankruptcy. In fact, in terms of box-office earnings, it came second only to *Snow White*. However, when *Alice in Wonderland* came out in 1951, it tanked at the box office and pushed the studio back into financial uncertainty. It got worse with *Peter Pan*, simply because audiences could not accept the deviations from the usual norms followed for portraying the story as a play. *Lady and the Tramp*, the first animated film that used CinemaScope, saw better reception upon its release in 1955, but it was still not enough to capture the fancy of audiences. Parallelly, the *Davy Crockett* miniseries and its compilation film were doing well, but it did not sit well with many who believed the eponymous hero was overrated. Disney now wanted to do something grand again to live up to the successes of *Snow White* and *Cinderella*. Using a massive six million dollars, he created *Sleeping Beauty*. Unfortunately for him, it failed to take off, too. This depressed Walt Disney so much that he stayed off the whole fairytale genre for quite some time. Interestingly, *One Hundred and One Dalmatians*, which was created with a far skimpier budget, became an instant hit when it was released in 1961.

That same year, Disney got approval from a financially struggling Pamela Lyndon Travers, better known as P.L. Travers, to make a film based on her *Mary Poppins* series. Disney had been chasing after Travers since 1938 for the rights to the series because his daughters had made him promise them that he would make a film on the character. But, until 1961, Travers had resisted his efforts out of fear that he would butcher her beloved character and ruin the story, especially since he was all for animation, which she detested. Even during the making of the film, there was friction between her and Disney over the depiction of the characters, especially Mary Poppins, the inclusion and exclusion of plot points, the music, and the use of animation. The animosity was apparently never resolved, as Travers decided not to let the sequels be adapted for the screen. The film was released in 1964.[13]

The only other notable film that was released during Walt's lifetime was *The Sword in the Stone* in 1963, which did not find much favor with the public or critics. So, Walt decided to try and emulate the formula of *One Hundred and One Dalmatians*, i.e., use animal characters to catch the fancy of children. He started work on *The Jungle Book* soon after *The Sword in the Stone* released, but he did not live to see it become successful. It was the last film he worked on before his death, and it was released posthumously, a year after Disney's death. It is quite interesting to note that these films, which fall under the Disney Silver Age, may not have been very successful when they released, but they all went on to become cult classics later on. The animators who notably worked on these movies would go on to become Disney's most trusted employees, later even becoming directors. Except for Les Clark, who had been with Disney since 1927, the rest all joined around the time *Snow White* went into production. They later came to be known as Disney's Nine Old Men.[14,15,16,17]

---

[13] https://www.biography.com/news/walt-disney-mary-poppins

[14] http://www.softschools.com/timelines/disney_movies_timeline/389/

# Chapter 11: Disney, the Megabrand

Walt had always had an obsession with trains. This obsession had first manifested in his childhood, and it never really went away. When Walt moved into yet another house in the LA district of Holmby Hills in 1949, he decided to build his own miniature backyard railroad, which came to be called the Carolwood Pacific Railroad. It was inspired by the one in the home of Ward Kimball, one of his Nine Old Men. Walt named it *Lilly Belle* after his wife, and it is now housed in the Carolwood Barn Museum. By 1952, he was dreaming about building a pan-American traveling railroad show, consisting of dioramas made of miniature objects, that he had nicknamed "Disneylandia." When that plan did not materialize, he

---

[15] https://listverse.com/2012/11/05/top-10-ridiculous-disney-movie-flops/

[16] http://www.hollywood.com/movies/the-evolution-of-disney-films-from-snow-white-to-now-60557826/#/ms-22719/7

[17] https://www.historyextra.com/period/modern/walt-disney-history-behind-films-pocahontas-pearl-harbor-national-treasure-lincoln/

turned his attention to building a kind of amusement park on the sixteen acres owned by the studio opposite his Burbank premises on Riverside Drive. The drive behind this, like *Mary Poppins*, was once again his daughters. He had taken them on a Saturday afternoon to Griffith Park to play, and as he was looking out at them, he had the epiphany of creating an amusement park that the whole family could enjoy. He drew much inspiration from Tivoli Gardens, an amusement park in Copenhagen, Denmark. But as planning progressed, Disney soon realized that sixteen acres would be too small. So, Disney purchased a lot with 160 acres in Anaheim, 38 miles south of Burbank, adjacent to the Santa Ana Freeway and Harbor Boulevard that was being constructed.

Letting the Nine Old Men manage the studio, he formed WED Enterprises in December of 1952 to oversee the project, mainly to separate it from any association with the studio and bypass Roy's reluctance. For funding, he decided to start a show called *Disneyland*, which would serve the dual purpose of promotion and financing. After NBC and CBS rejected the proposal, Roy got ABC to broadcast the show, as well as provide money for the construction of the park in return for a portion of the ownership. The success in getting ABC on board is credited in part to ABC's newbie status in the entertainment world and in part to Walt's artist friend Herbert Ryman, who spent a whole weekend in September of 1953, known as the "lost weekend," in a closed room with Walt, as Walt gave instructions and Ryman made a carbon pencil rendering of Walt's dream park on paper. This artist's impression of the aerial view of Disneyland is what is said to have convinced the network. However, both Roy and Lillian were quite worried. Walt was still pouring a lot of money from his own pocket into the making of *Disneyland* because the studio shareholders were reluctant and unsure of its success for a long time. But Walt did not care—he wanted his park to be the best. So, he hired engineers as well as animators, calling them his "Imagineers," to work on the project through WED Enterprises. Walt made his men study every theme park design and the way they operated in the US firsthand. Construction began in July 1954, and on July 17th, 1955, after an expenditure of seventeen million dollars, Disneyland was opened to the public. There were only between thirteen to twenty attractions back then, which has grown manifold by now. The park had an oblong pear shape, circled by the Disneyland Railroad. Main Street connected all its sections and was inspired by the Main Street of Marceline, where Disney's interest in trains was first engendered. The opening, though, was a bit rocky. For one, the opening day had been invitation-only, with only 6,000 tickets printed. But counterfeit tickets were printed, and so, attendance reached 28,000. A plumbers' strike forced Disney to choose running toilets over functional drinking fountains, vendors ran out of food, a gas leak forced one of the park's four sections, Fantasyland, to be closed, and wet paint and soft asphalt caused inconveniences to guests. Yet, by the end of the year, about 3.6 million guests had gone to the park.[18,19,20]

Disneyland was not the last park he was responsible for. Disney realized his park was attracting only five percent of people from the eastern part of the USA, even though the majority of the American population lived there. So, around 1958, he decided to build another park on that side of the country. However, he did not want it to be just another amusement park. He was planning to build a futuristic city based on which all future cities could be planned. Walt started calling it the Experimental Prototype Community of Tomorrow or EPCOT. He built a large number of ghost subsidiary companies to buy land in Bay Lake, Florida, which is located near Orlando. He even kept his name secret to ensure that he got a low price for the

---

[18] https://www.telegraph.co.uk/films/0/walt-disney-disneyland-bizarre-true-stories-conspiracy-theories/

[19] https://www.pbs.org/wgbh/americanexperience/features/reinventing-american-amusement-park/

[20] https://www.designingdisney.com/parks/disneyland-resort/construction-disneyland/

land. Initially, the plan had been for 10,000 acres, but it had ballooned to over 30,000 by the end. The project was finally revealed to the public in 1965 after a slip-up to an *Orlando Sentinel* reporter.[21] However, even before construction began, Walt passed away in 1966, just ten days after he turned 65. Roy Disney was all but retired by then, but he decided to come out of retirement to fulfill Walt's last dream. The entire project took six years to complete, and it was modeled more on a resort than a city ahead of its time. Walt Disney World may have opened posthumously in Orlando, Florida, on October 1st, 1971, by the efforts of Roy, but it had Walt's vision written all over it. Contrary to popular belief, Walt's body is not kept cryogenically frozen beneath Disneyland. He was cremated, and the ashes rest at Forest Lawn Memorial Park in California.

Walt's influence was not restricted just to the entertainment world. He was also a consultant to the 1959 American National Exhibition in Moscow, contributed four exhibits to the 1964 New York World's Fair, acted as chairman in the 1960 Winter Olympics ceremonies, and also collaborated with NASA on the "Man in Space" episode of the *Disneyland* series. Even after his death, the films created by his studio are the highest earners in the world, with some of the best animated, as well as live-action films, in its pocket.[22]

---

[21] https://www.themeparkinsider.com/flume/201312/3819/

[22] https://en.wikipedia.org/wiki/Walt_Disney

# Conclusion

Walt Disney died of lung cancer on December 15th, 1966, less than a month after he was diagnosed and in spite of using the latest treatment of cobalt therapy on him. At that time, there was a deluge of people flooding to Disney's creations—240 million saw his movies, 100 million more his TV programs, 80 million bought Disney merchandise, and 7 million went to Disneyland in solidarity. Walt holds the record of 59 Academy Award nominations and 22 Oscars, a record yet to be broken by a single man. He was the man responsible for carrying the animation world to where it is today, and even now, he is an inspiration for any artist. His innovation was recognized by reputed institutions all across the world, including Harvard, Yale, and UCLA. He has two stars at the Hollywood Walk of Fame. He also created the California Institute of the Arts from the LA Conservatory of Music and Chouinard.[23]

But perhaps the biggest contribution of Walt Disney lies in creating a brand that captured the imagination of people across age groups, nations, and cultures. He made fairytale princess stories in vogue again, and even today, people wait with bated breath whenever Disney Studios announces a film. A person lives on through the

---

[23] https://en.wikipedia.org/wiki/Walt_Disney

legacy they leave behind, and the legacy of Disney is one whose true extent can never be fathomed.

It cannot be denied that he had his faults. In fact, there were many. He often treated his men badly in his insane drive to realize his vision, he was somewhat egotistical, and at many times in history, his narrow outlook resulted in him being seen in a bad light. While these are not ignorable, they can, in no way, undermine the obvious instinct he had for knowing what would take the world by storm. His was the quintessential rags-to-riches story, the realization of the American Dream in the truest sense. Perhaps, one day, another like him may be born. But his are pretty large shoes to fill. After all, Walt Disney was the original greatest showman, a title that can never be taken from him.

# Check out another Captivating History book

# For Future Reading

Barrier, Michael. *The Animated Man: A Life of Walt Disney*. April 30, 2017. University of California Press.

Susanin, Timothy S. *Walt Before Mickey: Disney's Early Years 1919-1928*. April 7, 2011. University Press of Mississippi.

Brian Burnes, Robert W. Butler, and Dan Viets. *Walt Disney's Missouri: The Roots of a Creative Genius*. June 1, 2002. Kansas City Star Books.

www.ingramcontent.com/pod-product-compliance
Lightning Source LLC
LaVergne TN
LVHW041648060526
838200LV00040B/1760